THE 30-MINUTE WRITER

HOW TO WRITE & SELL SHORT PIECES

THE 30-MINUTE WRITER

WRITER

HOW TO WRITE & SELL SHORT PIECES

CONNIE EMERSON

Writer's
Digest
Books

Cincinnati, Ohio

This hardcover edition of *The 30-Minute Writer: How to Write and Sell Short Pieces* features a "self-jacket" that eliminates the need for a separate dust jacket. It provides sturdy protection for your book while it saves paper, trees and energy.

97 96 95 94 93   5 4 3 2 1

Library of Congress Cataloging in Publication Data

Emerson, Connie
    The 30-minute writer : how to write and sell short pieces / Connie Emerson. — 1st ed.
         p.   cm.
    Includes index.
    ISBN 0-89879-538-9
    1. Authorship.   I. Title.
PN147.E44   1993
808'.02 — dc20   92-38405
                                                                         CIP

Edited by Jack Heffron
Designed by Carol Buchanan

Pages vi-vii constitute an extension of this copyright page.

To Ralph H. Emerson

Permissions

Table of Contents

I. GETTING IT TOGETHER . . . 3

Time is precious. Take your *time*, for instance. In order to stretch it, you have to make every minute count. This chapter teaches you shortcut techniques for coming up with great ideas, shows you how to keep your thoughts in order, and shows you how to zero in on the short forms that will bring you the longest returns — both in money and satisfaction. Whether you have thirty minutes each day or only two hours on Sunday afternoons, you won't have to spend your time wondering where to begin.

II. SHORT TAKES . . . 9

You say you're the sort of person who likes to know a little bit about a lot of things. Then these pieces, which can be read at a glance and written in minutes, may be your fast way to make a writing buck.

III. ONE-PAGERS . . . 24

Jump starts. Flash finishes. Zippy sentences in between. Those ingredients go into the 500 to 1,000 word articles that are today's best-sellers. Readers don't want to waste a lot of time getting their information. After you've read this chapter, you won't want to waste any time, either, getting to your word processor.

IV. THE NOT-SO-WELL-DEVELOPED PERSONALITY . . . 41

Miniprofiles of 700 words or less are a lot easier to write than multifaceted personality pieces. Faster, too. This chapter shows you how to cut research and writing time while effectively capturing your subject's persona on paper.

V. SOUNDING OFF . . . 58

Giving people a piece of your mind can be profitable as well as psychologically gratifying. Whether you're pro-free prophylactics or anti-animal research; bent on saving the rain forests or doing away with drug dealers, the world can be your soapbox when you write op-ed pieces that sell. Get the how-to-do-it message in this chapter.

VI. LAUGHING MATTER . . . 74

Funny thing about humor, it reads easy but is hard to write. However, if you're clever, you can learn to arrange your words so that editors smile as they write the checks that will keep you laughing all the way to the bank.

VII. HOT TIPS . . . 90

You're the neighborhood Heloise, the town's Mary Ellen. You've devised seven thousand practical uses for plastic meat trays and have revolutionized spring cleaning so that it's a one-hour gala. You would like to share your secrets with everyone but can't figure out how. Hint: Read this chapter.

VIII. POSITIVELY INSPIRATIONAL . . . 104

Yesterday they were called inspirationals. Now they're known as brighteners. Whatever you call them, if you're able to write a few words that will give your readers hope and make a dark day brighter, you'll inspire editors to say yes. This chapter shows you how.

IX. DINING FOR DOLLARS . . . 120

You can have your cake and eat it too when you're a restaurant reviewer. Not only will you go home with boxes full of extra food, you'll find that writing the reviews won't take much longer than it does to eat your dinner. That is, if you thoroughly digest the tidbits in this chapter.

XV. PROSE: A STRING OF PEARLS

First you write one article; then another. Soon you have a whole string of them—sometimes all on the same theme or different aspects of a single subject. Maybe you land a job writing weekly columns. It's time to start thinking about putting your already written work together in a book, an anthology. Maybe a syndicated column. This chapter looks at your options.

Introduction

THE 30-MINUTE WRITER

The dynamics of magazine writing have changed dramatically during the past decade. Style is brighter, snappier. Simple sentences with far fewer clauses predominate. Tight writing is the rule.

Magazine formats have changed as well. Much more space is devoted to short articles and items. In several magazines, new departments that contain short freelance pieces have been inaugurated. One of the most obvious magazine trends has been toward more front-of-the-book briefs, many of which are contributed by freelancers.

These magazines mirror society, for we, too, have changed in the past ten years. We have more options, new life-styles. Less time to squeeze in everything we want to do.

It's an ideal time for people who would like to write — but don't have lots of uninterrupted time — to break into the market. *The 30-Minute Writer* shows you how.

The 30-Minute Writer explores the premise that all of us who would like to write simply don't have uninterrupted hours to devote to writing. More likely, we have fifteen minutes here, a half-hour there, and don't have the same bits and pieces available each day.

But it is possible to produce publishable material by working in fits and starts — especially if you concentrate on writing shorter items such as miniprofiles, front-of-the-book short takes, reviews, one-page articles, op-eds, personal essays and recipes. Fortunately for us, no time in the history of magazines has been more conducive to this kind of writing.

This book, however, not only features the most marketable of today's short forms, it also goes into the process of producing them, providing a sort of game plan for each of the various kinds of writing. These plans of attack divide the steps in the writing process—whether for a review, a recipe or a miniprofile—into work segments of thirty minutes or less.

Such plans, for me, are crucial, since in order to make the time fragments and thirty-minute sessions count, it's necessary to use the time efficiently. That means organization. That also means that idea generation and phrase making can (and sometimes *must*) go on while we're involved in pursuits other than writing. For the 30-Minute Writer, any segment of time—no matter how small—can be productive.

In sum, *The 30-Minute Writer* is a practical guide that tells you about the various short forms and shows you how to use your time most effectively. This book reflects my own experience as a freelancer. It also offers suggestions and examples from a wide variety of freelancers, editors and contesters. As a writer who has never been able to sit still for long stretches and who writes at odd hours, I'm really enthusiastic about the "thirty-minute" concept. I'm sure you will be, too.

CHAPTER I
Getting It Together

Some writers seem to have all the time in the world. They're the types you read about in novels. You know, the ones who have villas on Ibiza complete with significant others who do their research (as well as Maria and Jose to fix dinner and prune the climbing roses).

But you're *real*. You teach school or manage a dress shop or work at the post office. Perhaps you have a family, too. Life is a clock race.

You've always liked to write. Wanted to be a writer. With free time coming only in bits and snatches, though, you've almost given up the dream.

Don't.

You can write no matter how limited your discretionary time may be. How do I know? Because my time often comes in bits and snatches, too.

I also have a skittery mind—one that blithely jumps from one unrelated thought to another—so it's difficult to concentrate on a single subject for very long. As a result, I'm not very good at applying the "seat of my pants to the seat of the chair" dictum. About fifteen or twenty minutes into a project and I'm off to pick up the cleaning or pick some wildflowers, then back again for another session at the word processor. It's like that almost every day. But those fifteen-, twenty- and thirty-minute scraps of time do add up.

A short pause here while you protest that you don't have a minute to spare.

If that's really the case, you better put this book down right now and give it to a friend who does. But chances are you do have some free time. You just don't realize it. And if you want to write badly enough, you'll find those elusive minutes.

You might try getting up half an hour earlier or going to bed half an hour later. Spend your lunch hour researching instead of window shopping. And consider using the time when the clothes are swishing around at the Laundromat or the poodle's being clipped or Jennifer is struggling with "Minuet in G" while you're waiting outside the piano teacher's house in the car.

It's what I call "throwaway time": those minutes and hours during each day when you're doing something that doesn't—or, at least, shouldn't—demand your whole attention.

For instance, I feel that physical exercise is one of the most important parts of my life, so five or six times a week I ride a stationary bicycle for thirty minutes. Now as far as boredom is concerned, most people I know regard riding an exercise bicycle right up there with watching soup simmer. But for me, those two and a half to three hours a week are valuable thinking time.

One day, while my feet are pedaling, I direct my mind to the problem of how to begin the article I'm currently putting together. The next day, I focus on composing a query letter. The third exercise session of the week may be devoted to thinking up recipes for the California Prune Festival Cook-Off. And so it goes.

The half hour or more most of us spend every now and then in beauty salons or barbershops is another example of throwaway time, time when we have a choice of what to do with our minds. Do we want to chat idly with whomever is working on our hair? Sit in silence and think about nothing in particular? Or do we take that time and use it constructively to further our writing careers?

I choose the third option. While the hairdresser is cutting or blow-drying my hair, I ask her questions. "What is the hardest part of being a working mother?" "How do you minimize jealousy among the three girls in your (blended) family?" "Where do you like to go camping?" "What kinds of articles do you like to read?" I tune in on problems, aspirations, pet peeves, and in the process come up with all sorts of article ideas as well as material I can use in writing them.

The most difficult part of making use of throwaway time, I realize, is maintaining focus. Some days, it's impossible to keep your mind on constructing a knock-their-socks-off lead or to stay zeroed in on how you're going to structure the restaurant review you have an assignment to write.

When that's the case, don't fight it. Try, instead, to do planning, bill paying, letter writing or other tasks that aren't related to writing but that will—if you don't do them now—use up some other part of the day's time. Then appropriate the released time for writing.

During an eighteen-month period not long ago, as an eight-to-fiver who banked a paycheck every two weeks, I continued to freelance in my spare minutes. Of course, I wasn't able to produce as many manuscripts as I do when I am freelancing full time, but I did manage to sell about forty-five newspaper and magazine articles plus a variety of shorter items during that year and a half.

Which brings us to the second premise of this book. It's lots easier to be successful as a 30-Minute Writer if you concentrate on writing the short forms, such as news briefs, one-page articles, short profiles, op-eds, short humor, hints and tips, "brighteners" (they used to be called inspirationals), reviews, recipes, personal essays, children's pieces and anecdotes.

It goes without saying that, although the "right" word you need to complete a 50-word tip may elude you for days, writing short forms generally takes a lot less time than putting together full-length articles.

There are other benefits as well. Beginning writers will find that fillers and short pieces open editorial office doors. It's often the only way a writer who hasn't written for a publication can make that initial sale. The editors' reasoning makes a lot of sense, once you've thought about it. A new writer is an unknown quantity.

Will she deliver what she has promised in her query?

His idea is great, but will he be able to sustain the reader's interest for 2,000 words?

Will she meet the deadline?

Will he send the piece at all?

By first purchasing short pieces or fillers, the editor can allay these fears, risking a minimum of money and editorial space.

For established writers, short forms can mean a change of pace (and grocery money) while they're devoting most of their time to a larger work, such as a novel or a company's biography.

Then consider the psychological advantages. For novices, composing a full-blown feature may appear as big a job as shoveling the snow off Red Square; a smaller bit of prose seems more possible to complete. There's also the matter of rejection. For beginner and pro alike, it's a lot easier to take when you haven't invested hours and hours of blood, sweat and research in the project.

It's possible, too, as we will see in chapter fifteen, to string work produced during short stretches of writing time together into full-length features and even books. After all, three hours spent writing on each of five days equals the same amount of time as thirty daily half-hour sessions.

MAXIMIZING YOUR MINUTES

The secret is to take the time you have — however brief — and use it wisely. What can you do in only thirty minutes? It will take just a sec to tell you. For instance, you can:

1. Generate (and write down) fifteen to twenty article ideas
2. File a three-inch-high pile of documents
3. Compose (or at least rough draft) a query letter
4. Type or word process three query letters and envelopes
5. Conduct an interview for a short profile
6. Research
7. Make information-gathering telephone calls
8. Gather materials on a subject you plan to write about
9. Bookkeeping (balance your business checking account,

work on your income tax, write any letters requesting payment of overdue accounts)

10. Type five letters requesting information and the accompanying envelopes (include self-addressed stamped envelopes for speedier responses)

11. Map out a master plan for your project, especially if it is 900 words or longer

At the outset, with pen and paper or word processor at hand, divide the project into segments such as planning, assembling materials, research, interviews, writing, packaging. Then estimate how much total time each segment will require (as you gain experience, you'll become more accurate in estimating time requirements).

It won't take much time—and it will make the job even more manageable—to draw up an organizational checklist. That way, you can jump quickly into each project without rummaging around in a pile of papers to find out what you need to do next. And don't underestimate the motivation to continue that you get each time you check an item off the list.

When I'm working on an article of 1,000 words, for example, and have only fragmented time in which to produce it, I begin with a planning session. Then I make a work schedule for myself. It may look something like this:

I.   Library research
  a. Check newspaper files
  b. See if there is any reference to subject in books, magazines, other printed sources
  c. Gather background info on people to be interviewed
II.   Interviews
  a. Make appointments with interviewees (either to meet in person or talk by telephone)
  b. Formulate lists of questions
  c. Actual interviews
  d. Transcribing notes on word processor
III. Writing

    a.   Rough draft
    b.   Polishing
  IV.   Illustrations
    a.   Taking any required photos
    b.   Obtaining them from other sources
  V.   Packaging
    a.   Writing cover letter
    b.   Making photocopies of cover letter and manuscript (if they have been written on typewriter)
    c.   Preparing photo caption sheets
    d.   Preparing self-addressed stamped envelope
    e.   Entering submission information in notebook or some other record-keeping device
    f.   Filing research information pertaining to the piece
    e.   Mailing the manuscript
12. Buy stamps, envelopes and other office supplies

    You will quickly find that many of the tasks in a 30-Minute Writer's life, such as preparing the self-addressed stamped envelopes, take only minutes if you have the necessary supplies on hand.

If you're able to get into the habit of utilizing each block of free time, no matter how small, you'll soon start making big strides along the path to becoming a 30-Minute Writer par excellence.

CHAPTER II

Short Takes

ASAP is the acronym of the era. We've all seen articles called "Meals You Can Make in Minutes" and "Skirts You Can Sew in an Hour." And what about the ads? "Teach Yourself Spanish in Ten Days," "Lose Inches in a Week." Contemporary society is obsessed with doing everything in a hurry.

It's no wonder, then, that the most dramatic change in magazines in the past decade has been the length of their articles. Not only have features become shorter, the trend toward printing multiple miniarticles—usually, but by no means always, at the quickest-to-turn-to front of the book—means that readers can scan those pages and learn things *fast*.

Called "short takes" or "briefs," these articles typically run from 200 to 400 words long, but they're often a good deal shorter. Writing is straightforward—nothing cute, nothing complicated. You would have a tough time editing any words out of these pieces, especially the shorter ones. With space so limited, each word must say precisely what you mean. Focus is sharp, with no room for material that's even the slightest bit extraneous.

A good example of this short form is the following which appeared in the "Palm Latitudes" department of *Los Angeles Times Magazine*. It's called "Chow" and was written by Janey Milstead.

Hungry for Russian caviar, or pate de foie gras, or one of 15 lobster dishes? Then pull up a menu. Price is no object. The caviar is only 35 cents, the pate 45. Is this Food Heaven? No, the Rare Book Room of the downtown Los Angeles Public Library, where a collection of local menus reflects the city's changing palate. Not surprisingly, bills o'fare well into the '30s and '40s present a plenitude of then-local seafood and a paucity of items now *de rigueur* on any menu. Chicken, for example, was scarce, and it wasn't cheap. Early Angelenos were also not into desserts—after-dinner tastes leaned more toward cheeses. Wines were neither plentiful nor regional, but the price was right—in 1912, a bottle of G.H. Mumms Extra Dry was $5. The avocado debuted in 1929 at the Hotel Alexandria, selling for a whopping $1, right up there with Russian caviar. A 1938 Tick Tock Tea Room showed an early health-consciousness with a fresh vegetable plate that still topped its chart 30 years later.

A trek through L.A. menus is also a good barometer of the buck—note how when the '80s hit, prices begin to skyrocket. Musso & Frank's broiled chicken, which opened the decade at $6.15, closed at twice the price. And, at the other end of the food chain, dinner at Knott's Berry Farm Fried Chicken Restaurant was $2.25 in 1955 and is now $9.45.

Inflation is, at least, democratic.

You'll notice that the subject—the collection of local menus in the Rare Book Room of the downtown Los Angeles Public Library reflects the city's changing palate and prices—is one that could in all probability support a longer article. However, Milstead has made it into an ideal nucleus for a short-short piece by keeping her intro short and clever, then providing illustrations for the article's premise—all in a mere 248 words. And how about that five-word close for sparkling efficiency?

Publications as diverse as *Outside* and *Cook's* have initiated a variety of "information at a glance" departments. While some of these shorties are staff written, many of them are by freelancers. That's great news for the 30-Minute Writer.

Not only do you need to do less research (which definitely means you can do it in bits and pieces of time), a couple hundred words doesn't take long to write once you have your information at hand.

Then add another big plus. Your notes and article-in-progress won't take up much space, so you can take them along with ease when you know you'll have some minutes to spare in the course of your day's routine.

Once you've read a number of these short items, you'll realize that research is minimal. Some of these miniarticles require no more than a phone call for all the information you'll need. But there is a potential trap here: inaccurate or heavily slanted information.

When you're researching a longer article, you interview a variety of people and read a number of documents. You're able to resolve—or at least mention in your piece—conflicts in information about the subject. The short piece doesn't give you that luxury. Since not all sources are reliable, you have to be darn sure that yours are before you write what you have been told. And even the most reliable sources are, by nature, as subjective as the rest of us.

MARKETING BRIEF

Finding markets for short subjects requires actually going through magazines in search of them, since they're usually not mentioned in *Writer's Market* or other marketing sources. This isn't much of a job, though, since they are easily identifiable. It's important, however, to check magazines frequently as an increasing number are adding short subjects to their editorial mixes as fast as they can effect format changes.

The trend toward miniarticles, which accelerated dramatically during the late 1980s and early 1990s, was part of a mass movement among magazines to update images—altering format, typeface, article content (shape, style and structure) to reflect the times.

A case in point is *Bon Appetit*, which at the beginning of 1991 completed its transformation. In the process of reshaping the magazine, several new sharply focused departments were inaugurated, including one called "Bon Vivant."

A potpourri of short items relating to food, dishes, cookbooks and kitchen implements, the Bon Vivant pages have a "now" look, with snappy typeface and lots of photos and drawings. Other publications, such as *Philadelphia Magazine*, which featured short takes long before they became trendy, have made these pages more prominent in their magazines' formats by such devices as repositioning and updating layouts.

Short takes are printed in virtually all kinds of publications. You'll find page after page of short bylined items in *Sports Afield*, or an occasional short piece on the outdoors in *Backpacker* that is followed by the writer's name. The fact that short items are bylined doesn't always mean they're written by freelancers, though, so it's a good idea to check bylines against the names on the masthead when you're analyzing a magazine for the first time.

Several departments in *Health*—among them "Nutrition," "Kids" and "Medical"—include bylined items. By masthead checking, however, you'll find that most names belong to staffers.

This shouldn't be a complete deterrent. There's always the chance that staffers are forced to come up with items because the publication doesn't receive enough suitable material from freelancers. Since short takes are a relatively new phenomenon in many publications, only the alert writers have perceived their importance as a market.

Although many short items don't require photos, it's not always the case—another reason for eyeballing the publications. Italicized print at the end of *Country Woman*'s "Out of the Attic" says, "Send us your favorite old photograph and the story behind it. You'll receive $100 if we publish it."

But most magazines don't spell out the necessity of including pictures. That's not a problem because you can pretty well determine by looking at back issues what sorts of items demand accompanying art.

MATCH PLAY

There are literally thousands of ideas floating around out there that would work well in short form. The trick is to decide which of those ideas are perfect for your targeted publications. And again, the only valid way you can make your decisions is by studying the magazines themselves. No two magazines have exactly the same requirements.

For example, freelancers are said to provide 90 percent of *Outside*'s copy, and a good deal of that material appears in short takes under various departments. One of these departments, "Dispatches," includes news, events and short profiles relevant to the outdoors.

Another, called "Destinations," tells about places to explore, travel news and tips for adventure travelers. The destinations can include any that might be of interest to the magazine's readers — wild horse sanctuaries, country inns, Arctic lakes.

"Review" evaluates products ranging from duffel bags to rock-climbing gear; "Expeditions" tells about adventures by bicycle, canoe, camel and other soft- or hard-adventure modes of travel. However, never take it for granted that the format/content/department requirements of *Outside* or any other magazine will remain static. Check your intended publications frequently to see if any changes have been made.

Though some of the items in these departments can run as long as 1,500 words, most of them are in the 200 to 600 word category. Best news of all is that *Outside* pays fifty cents a word for these little gems, which also offer the best way to break into the magazine.

Here's an example titled "Stargazing" that appeared in the "Almanac" department:

> March is a fine time to introduce children to Ursa Major, the Big Dipper, which will be directly overhead in its rotation around Polaris, the North Star. The full moon occurs on the 30th, the new moon on the 16th. Toward the end of the month, Mercury will be

visible low in the western sky at sunset. Two other planets can also be seen at sunset this month: Venus, shining brilliantly about 30 degrees above the western horizon, and Mars, in the constellation Taurus, high in the southern sky. Saturn, the fourth and last planet visible to the unaided eye, is in the constellation Capricorn and will stand about 15 degrees above the southeastern horizon a few hours before sunrise. The vernal equinox, marking the start of spring, occurs on the 21st at 3:02 A.M. Greenwich mean time. That's 10:02 P.M. eastern standard time on the 20th — so you won't have to get up in the wee hours if you want to celebrate.

That's about 165 words worth of information on a subject most any competent writer could research in a half hour — provided she had read the magazine, got the idea, and knew about how much information she would need. Amateur astronomers could put their facts together in even less time.

And the little articles may bring you more than money. *Outside* and many other publications listed in *Writer's Market* acknowledge that selling short items is the fastest way for a writer to get his foot in the editorial door. Sell about a half-dozen short items during the course of a year to the editor of almost any magazine and he'll recognize your name as a writer to be counted on. Add that name recognition to a good query for a feature article on an appropriate subject and you're on the way to a major sale.

Short items, like feature articles, are a reflection of the magazine's readership. The more specialized the magazine, the more narrowly focused its briefs. For instance, *Sports Afield's* short items focus on fishing spots like Florida's phosphate pits and the Salmon River in New York; about duck decoys, muzzle loader maintenance, keeping warm, and any other subject of interest about hunting and fishing. Its readers might well be interested in keeping warm at football games as well as in the duck blind, but they buy the magazine because of their interest in rod and gun pursuits, so the editors keep material focused on those activities.

Not surprisingly, all the short pieces in *Travel-Holiday* have to do with travel. In one issue, "new & notable" showcased the ultimate travel compact, the hottest-ticket play in London's West End, a lightweight jacket that would be great for traveling, a restaurant in the Catskills, an oasis resort south of Marrakech, a traveling exhibit of paintings by the Fauves, cross-country skis, and Dublin as Europe's 1991 "City of Culture."

By contrast, *Los Angeles Magazine*'s readers aren't buying that magazine to find out about a special subject or pursuit. Some of them hunt and fish; others are animal rights activists. Many, but by no means all, of them travel. So while there may be an occasional short piece in the magazine on fishing in Los Angeles or one that has to do with travel, they're only facets of an eclectic array of information. The editors want to include enough variety in the content of the short takes so that their departments will be of interest to all of their readers.

The diversity of those readers is reflected in the magazine's short takes. "Finds" contains short bylined items with accompanying color photos that tell readers about things to buy—everything from humanely raised veal and secondhand custom-crafted boots to antique appraisals.

Most city and regional magazines use a lot of short items. One of the reasons is that many places and events in an area are worth writing about, but they aren't interesting/important enough to justify more than a paragraph or two. Or it may be merely a matter of space. *Los Angeles Magazine*, thick as it may be, simply doesn't have pages enough to cover everything in the megalopolis.

Although a few of the regionals, such as *Boston Magazine*, may use only an occasional sidebar or boxed item, many of them devote several pages to little pieces in each issue.

Midwest Living is one of them. Some of the items in the "Our Midwest Discoveries" department are staff written, but several on the two to three pages devoted to them each issue are bylined.

You'll notice one constant ingredient in all of the items: the link between their subjects and the Midwest. In one issue, for example, the Chicago branch of the National Archives; an Ohio family that produces custom-made baskets; a mining supershovel on display in Kansas; and a South Dakota mining tour were subjects of items ranging in length from 84 to 138 words, for which the magazine paid $25 each. Two months later, subjects included classic clocks in Iowa, a restaurant housed in an old Minnesota schoolhouse, and a plastics outlet in Wisconsin where a quarter-million yo-yos are sold each year.

In each issue of *Nevada* magazine a multipage department lists special events that will take place during the period according to region and date. On each page of the department, one or two of the events are written about in greater length. These items, which are boxed and usually include a photo, not only add to the attractiveness of the magazine's layout, they provide work for freelancers, too.

Don't assume that the geographic tie-in to places, products or events is the kind of material all of these regional magazines are looking for, however. In the same issue of *Mpls.-St. Paul* that featured short pieces on the results of a greeting card reaction study conducted by a University of Minnesota professor and on an inflated pig that appeared in the 1938 St. Paul Winter Carnival parade, the following short, called "Bon Verbiage" by John Addington, also appeared.

A confession from the wordmudgeon who frequently fulminates against new coinages: I like gigaflop. No, gigaflop is not a ballyhooed play that fails disastrously on Broadway. The super-computer people coined the word to describe how fast their machines can do stuff.

A gigaflop is a billion arithmetic calculations performed in one second. Already I can see noncomputer applications for this dandy word.

As I filed this column, the Hennepin County Board was considering its first billion-dollar budget. Imagine the headline possibilities: HENNCO BOARD EYES FIRST GIGABUDG!

The savings-and-loan scandal goes on, with taxpayers paying gigabucks to rectify gigafraud and hoping that judges will hand down at least a few gigayear sentences to the fraudulent.

Carl Sagan, who told us about billions and billions of celestial bodies on TV a few years ago, now can save his breath by switching to gigagalaxies.

Out at Paisley Park, Prince makes ever greater sums with his music and movies and concert tours. Soon he'll perform the world's first gigagig.

But now we've reached the bottom of the column. Gigathanks for reading it.

Travel magazines are another great short takes market. Again, the kind of material is as diverse as the destinations to which one can journey. *Caribbean Travel and Life* features bylined pieces that are about a column long. They're mostly about destinations, places to eat and vacation activities, but you'll also find short cookbook reviews as well as write-ups about other books related to travel.

"Motoroaming" in *MotorHome* consists of a half-dozen short pieces, written by both staff and freelancers. Subjects all relate in some way to motorhomes: the Recreational Vehicle/Mobile Home Hall of Fame in Elkhart, Indiana, for instance, or ultraelaborate campsites under construction in San Diego.

BIG IDEAS FOR LITTLE ITEMS

Coming up with salable ideas for your short items is something you can do in short order if you use recent issues of the magazines you hope to write for as your guide. Let's take a close look at *Bon Appetit*'s department "Bon Vivant." This will show how easy it is to think of things to write about.

The department—partially staff written—consists of as many as four pages, including photos and illustrations.

Mini-restaurant reviews, specialty foods such as truffles and fancy pastries, cookbooks, intimate hotels, gift wrap, wines, ski resorts, food-shaped jewelry, dishes and cutlery, herbs, mini-travel itineraries, cookware and cookware racks are all subject categories that have been written about in the past.

Chances are they'll be popular categories in the future, too. But before you start thinking of specialty foods produced in your area and furniture with a food motif, take a second look. It shows that the only items with bylines are almost always about restaurants and hotels.

Having narrowed down the possibilities, the next step is to see what kinds of hotels and restaurants are featured. It doesn't take long to determine that the hotels must be upscale—a posh Victorian inn in New Orleans with rates from $195 to $395, a French auberge, a small but grand hotel in Munich.

As far as the restaurants chosen in the past are concerned, you'll see at a glance that they're not of your neighborhood Holiday Inn dining room variety. In order to catch the editor's eye, you'll do best choosing places that are trendy, with smashing decor and featuring menu choices created from innovative combinations of ingredients.

The way I handle the next part of the idea process is by making lists. If I were aiming at "Bon Vivant," for instance, I would make two, labeled "Lodging Places" and "Restaurants." You notice that "Hotels" wasn't my choice as a heading. The reason is that it's a far more limiting word than one that includes not only traditional hotels, but also bed and breakfasts, resorts, inns and other places where paying guests can stay overnight. By keeping the lists in a place where you can readily get to them, jotting down appropriate ideas whenever they occur to you is a cinch.

You can use this same technique to generate ideas for any magazine's short takes. Be sure to write the name of the publication on every idea sheet, though, so that you won't have to remember which idea list is which after you've made dozens of them.

Because it *is* necessary to make these lists for every magazine you hope to write for. Don't assume, for example, that editors of all food magazines that use short takes like the same kinds of items. Although, like in *Bon Appetit*, the freelance items in *Eating Well* are also food-focused, they generally have a news peg and are more generic/less product oriented. As an example, here's "The Good-Nutrition Expedition," by Paul McCarthy.

Imagine the stamina needed to drag a sled loaded with 200

pounds of gear and provisions across the planet's coldest and windiest continent for four months in temperatures that drop as low as minus 50 degrees F.

For Minnesotan Ann Bancroft and a team of four women, no detail is left to the imagination as they finalize plans to be the first group to scale 1,700 miles of uncharted Antarctica terrain this fall with nothing but their own strength to propel them. No dogs or machinery will be used to pull the sleds; every food item taken along must fuel the adventurers' bodies efficiently without contributing excess weight to their loads.

Bancroft knows firsthand how intolerable expedition food can become—she ate three meals a day of fatty seal meat and butter-by-the-stick on an expedition to the North Pole in 1986. The high-fat foods seemed necessary at the time, providing the maximum amount of calories for the weight. But anxious to develop a more varied larder, Bancroft is working with Colorado dietitian Julie Ann Lickteig to include more "pantry" than packaged food this time.

The menu is loaded with foods high in complex carbohydrates: pasta, rice, dried potatoes, couscous and grains, with only 35 percent of calories derived from fattier salamis, precooked sausages, cheese and butter. Lickteig explains that a high-carbohydrate diet is more efficient at high altitudes—the climbers will be as high as 7,500 feet—since carbohydrates require less oxygen to digest than do the denser fats. But she predicts that the lower-fat diet and the high altitudes will require the climbers to drink at least four quarts of water each day. "They will spend 3 hours daily just melting snow," she says.

Katy Koontz, former *McCall's* travel editor and a freelancer for the past four years, says she gets lots of good ideas for short items by reading *USA Today*. "Even if a specific idea isn't the right one, that idea will make you think of similar ones. If the geographic area isn't right, you can apply the idea to an area that is. The important thing is that it gets you thinking." Koontz also advises writers to take ideas from their life experiences. "People don't always want to read about exciting or bizarre subjects. They want everyday information they can apply to their own lives."

ONE WORD AT A TIME

As we mentioned earlier, you simply can't afford to waste words when you're writing a short-short. Strunk and White's *Elements of Style* is about the best friend you can have when it comes to winnowing words as far as common phrases are concerned. In a handy section of the book, such phrases as "in a hasty manner" and "owing to the fact that" are listed along with their more word-efficient equivalents (hastily and since or because).

If you have problems with any of the other words, your thesaurus will be a great help. By looking at synonyms, you'll be able to choose the word with precisely the right nuance and thereby be able to say exactly what you mean in as few words as possible.

Style and structure vary with the publication, too. Those in *Working Woman Magazine*'s "Business Buzz" department often begin with one or two straightforward summary sentences. The first two in a 132-word short, which was not bylined, called "Jobs and Gender: Who's Satisfied?" set the stage for the information that followed this way:

> You don't need a formal study to know that most executives consider themselves underpaid and overworked. But new research shows that relationships with co-workers and challenging work can compensate.

In the same department of the same issue, the 215-word "Giving Transfers the Thumbs Down" by Robin Kamen began with these two sentences:

> Transfers were once considered a routine part of an executive's climb up the corporate ladder. But faced with a growing reluctance among employees, companies are looking for ways to let movers and shakers stay put.

Those two examples not only give astute magazine analysts an idea of one kind of lead the magazine's editors favor, they also reveal clues to the editor-friendly content — a traditional business fact of life that because of changing attitudes/life-styles is being challenged or modified.

Short items in *Omni* are written in a livelier style, with clever turns of phrase and literary devices galore. The leads are generally two or three sentences long, but the fact that the pieces are often under 200 words doesn't keep their authors from injecting personality into their work. Take this one called "The Fickle Fungi of France" by George Nobbe, which begins:

> In the French forests of Perigord, it is almost sacrilegious to trifle with the manner in which truffles are unearthed. Undaunted, a biochemist from the University of Manchester's Institute of Science and Technology in England has developed an electronic device that may give pink slips to the hounds and hogs used to find truffles.

Another shortie, called "Deja vu — Again," by Peggy Noonan, begins this way:

> If this sounds familiar, it just might be: Deja vu — that eerie feeling of remembering something that is happening right in front of your eyes — has been explained . . . again.

Yet a third example from the same magazine — this one "Food That Goes Bump in the Night" by Steve Nadis — illustrates that clever writing counts a lot at *Omni*:

> Sure, food can be pretty to look at and frequently pleasing to the palate, but can it dance? Not yet, at least not in public. But two researchers from RJR Nabisco have just patented what amounts to a volcanic cookie, which spews a lava-like filling from its center when heated in a microwave oven.

You won't find a predominant style or structure in the mini-pieces printed in *Self Magazine*. A glossary of moviemaking terms by Ellen Sherman, called "behind the camera: how to tell a grip from a gaffer" begins with an explanatory paragraph, then goes on to list eleven terms in boldface, such as "swing gang" and "focus puller," followed by their definitions in regular type.

"Help for the Winter Blues" by Michelle Nellett gives readers a paragraph of explanatory prose, followed by three bulleted tips. Other shorts the magazine has printed include a series of New Year's resolutions made by celebrities, and a chart chronicling rock stars' ages, home bases, stage M.O., quotable quotes and the like.

TOTAL SUBMISSION

Since it would take about the same amount of time to write a decent query letter as it takes to write a short piece, you don't query editors about short takes—another time-saver. In fact, writing short takes is so time-efficient you won't want to waste a moment more getting started. So do it now.

THE 30-MINUTE WRITER'S PLAN OF ACTION

1. Tear out or photocopy pages of short items as you read magazines. Since we assume that any person who wants to sell articles reads magazines, you really don't have to earmark any special time for this project. Be sure, though, to take the extra time to write the name of the publication if it isn't already on each sheet.

2. Be on the alert for new products (especially those made in your area), innovations, different ways of solving old problems, special exhibits, trends and the like. If you're quick enough in finding out about the first winery in an area where wine has never been produced before, for example, you're almost sure to have a salable short item idea.

3. On a regular basis, pair up publications and ideas. Make

a checklist for each of them regarding the information you will need and possible sources of that information.

4. After you have the necessary information down on paper, write a rough draft of each item, polish it and pop it in the mail.

CHAPTER III
One-Pagers

Next time you have thirty minutes to spare, leaf through copies of magazines from ten or twenty years ago. You'll be amazed at how different they are from issues the same magazines published today. Content—and the way it is treated—has changed dramatically. The colors in the photos and ads are brighter, clearer. Formats have been updated.

The most significant change, however—as we mentioned in the preceding chapter—has been in magazine article length. Long before short takes became the editorial rage, feature articles started getting shorter. Whereas 2,000 word lengths were common in the 1970s, by the early 1980s most articles were at least 500 words shorter. Many of them, as a matter of fact, were 1,000 words and less. By the end of the 1980s, the trend toward one-pagers had become well established.

Simply put, one-pagers are short articles that—along with accompanying photos or other art—fit on a single page. This means they must be no longer than 1,000 words or, if there are two or three pictures, even shorter. Focus is, of necessity, narrow; telling about one breed of show horses or one facet of their training, for example, rather than about horses in general. Sentences and paragraphs usually are short; descriptive words, concise.

The short article trend shows strong signs of continuing. It's a function of that "let me know about it, but do it in a hurry" syndrome.

This one-pager philosophy is immediately apparent when you glance through United Airline's in-flight magazine, *Vis a Vis*. Almost every one of the publication's articles — ranging in scope from business pieces to celebrity profiles — takes up no more than a single page, including photos.

While most magazines don't utilize the one-pager to the extent that *Vis a Vis* does, more and more of them are devoting an increasing proportion of editorial copy to shorter pieces.

As far as the reader is concerned, this one-page format gives enough details about a subject to make him or her feel informed but not deluged. It also precludes the nuisance of having to turn to page 84 or 123 or even to the next editorial page (a real hassle in magazines full of ad supplements that aren't paginated) to read the rest of an article.

For 30-Minute Writers, the one-page piece is a marvelous option. Not only does it take less time than the longer pieces to write, it's usually quicker to research. And the low psychological hazards of producing a manuscript that's only three double-spaced pages long greatly decrease the beginning writer's fear of trying.

As an established writer, I like the one-pager for yet another reason. When I'm working on a book or on a major article that takes a good deal of effort, it's refreshing to write shorter pieces as a change of pace. Turnaround time is much faster, so you get jolts of gratification that keep you enthusiastic about the longer works in progress.

While I have been writing this book, for example, I've also queried editors about several one-pagers. So far, checks have come in for two 800-word pieces on festivals, a 900-word piece on shuttle boats, and four newspaper articles of 1,000 words or less. The articles haven't taken long to write or research and have made that daily trip to the mailbox much more gratifying.

For any writer, the piece that's 1,000 words or less can also be more profitable to write than the longer ones, in terms of the ratio of time spent to money earned. In the first place, you can't cover all aspects of most subjects in the one-pager's allotted words, so the amount of research you have to do is much less. Secondly, you won't have to spend nearly as much time writing.

That is, if you use the initial thirty-minute segments of your writing time to become familiar with the markets that will be easiest for you to write for and to carefully think out your projects.

Of course, the short article form does have drawbacks. Focus must be *very* tight. You'll have to be extremely economical with your words (something that's especially difficult for many beginning writers), and you probably won't be able to treat your subject as fully as you would like. My solution, when confronted with these problems, is to ask, Do these words *really* have to be included—even though I like them a lot? or, Which would I rather do—leave this extra marvelous information in the article when I send it to the editor and risk a rejection, or cut and slash so it will be accepted?

INFORMATION LOCATION

Becoming familiar with the markets and the kinds of one-pagers that various publications use is vital. The more magazines you're acquainted with, the better your chances of finding one or two or half a dozen that mesh with your interests and writing ability.

When you have limited time to spend, it's pretty silly to try to write for a magazine whose audience is primarily made up of physicians if the magazine's subject matter is exclusively about medicine. That is, unless you have a medical background and don't have to start at square one learning about your subject.

As a person whose interest in and knowledge of economics is marginal, to say the least, I found this lesson out by painful experience when I wrote an article on slot machine leasing for a business publication. Researching and writing the piece took three times as long as it should have because I had to learn so much basic information before I could begin to write.

On the other hand, if, like me, you're interested in leisure-time activities, writing for a magazine for physicians or economists that focuses on travel or sports is a natural.

By the same token, you may be uncomfortable writing for magazines whose style is academic or publications whose articles are filled with contemporary slang. The time to find compatible publications is before you begin to write. It's rough to discover your incompatibility halfway through the piece.

There are several ways to obtain marketing information, and you shouldn't overlook any of them.

Writer's Market, for example, lists more than 1,700 article markets. These listings contain such information as the publications' names and addresses, the names of their editors, circulation size, rate of payment and editorial requirements—usually including word length.

When I'm searching for markets, I use *Writer's Market* for bedtime reading, armed with different colored highlighter marking pens and bookmarks. I've established a color code: blue is for articles of 1,000 words or less; orange is for anecdotes; yellow is for reviews; and so on. Each night, I go through a section of the book, marking each listing's categories that interest me. You can set up a similar method of your own. Whatever works best for you is the right system.

If the magazines that interest you aren't available at the newsdealer's, send for sample copies from the publisher. This is necessary because reading about markets just isn't enough. It's also important to study the magazines for content and style.

Visit newsstands every month or so, because dozens of magazines debut each year. Ask friends to save their old magazines for you, since many good markets are publications that are sent only to people who have accounts at certain banks, hold insurance policies underwritten by certain companies or are members of automobile clubs, fraternal or occupation-related organizations.

Public and university library periodicals departments are other important sources of marketing information, since they subscribe to dozens of magazines. Laundromats and doctors', dentists' and repair shops' waiting rooms are places you'll find publications you might otherwise not see. Libraries in many areas have "give-away" magazine tables or boxes. Take home an armful and clip out articles that are similar to the kinds you would like to write.

FOCUS ON IDEAS

All clichés aside, the sky's the limit as far as subjects for one-pagers are concerned. You want to write about miniature paintings or memory training. Why not! Your interests may be in mathematics or history. Great! Since publications are directed toward people with just about every vocation and avocation, almost any idea that's fresh, that can be scaled to size, and that is compatibile with the times, will work.

Freshness comes from using an approach that isn't hackneyed and timeworn. Even though hundreds of short articles have been written about car maintenance, innovative writers are still able to think of different ways to look at the subject. "Coaching Your Car to Pass Its Emissions Test," "Nervous About On-the-Road Breakdowns?" and "Keeping an Old Car Looking Like a Youngster" are only a few ways you can breathe new life into old subjects.

You can evaluate the idea's scope by considering a couple of factors. Does the subject have depth, will you run out of things to say about it after you've written 300 words? Or is it so broad that you'll need at least 1,500 to do it justice? If it's too broad, could you cut a sliver out of the subject pie and write about it?

Perhaps you're an animal lover and want to write short articles about your canine, equine and feline friends. But what can you say in just a page? It's hardly enough room for a piece about a single species, let alone the whole animal kingdom. So what you have to do is cut your subject down to size. For example, write about an interesting breed—say, miniature horses. Or pick some aspect of pet care—like health, nutrition or exercise—and write about it.

That's exactly what Margaret Connelly Nicholson did in her piece, "Keeping your pet out of jail . . . Get the scoop on animal laws," which appeared in *First*. The piece, divided into an introduction and five subheaded sections, hits the high spots of pet ownership vs. the law. It talks about such subjects as peace-disturbing pets, "pup-ternity" suits, biters and burrowers without wasting one of its 583 words.

As far as timeliness is concerned, be sure that the idea is not so avant-garde that people will have difficulty relating to it, but not so much in the mainstream that it's been overdone. Other highly salable subject qualities are broad appeal and human interest. Editors reject many good ideas because, while they would interest a segment of the magazine's readership, that segment isn't large enough to justify the article.

Finally, in vetting your ideas, decide whether you need to be specially qualified to write about them. If you really like an idea, but haven't the necessary qualifications to write about it, can you readily find an authority on the subject to collaborate with you?

Think about style as well. Would your subject be showcased best in a piece filled with adjectives, anecdotes or long quotes — all devices that use a lot of words — or can the story be told simply?

ONE-PAGER TYPES

As you study the magazines, you will find that many one-pagers are the kind of articles known as "evergreens." They're about timeless subjects, such as Christmas traditions or historic events/sites. Although their purpose also may be to entertain, these pieces are, for the most part, informational. They add to the reader's body of general knowledge.

Contemporary subjects also make for editorially desirable one-pagers. When there's a boom in secondhand store shopping or a new sport such as rollerblading becomes popular, readers want to learn enough about the subject so that they can feel "informed."

Along with general-interest publications, magazines that highlight travel, sports, business and health are among the hot test markets today for informational one-pagers.

The short travel articles that sell best focus on a single place or event — from a small hotel on Maui to a national park in Australia; from a sing-along Messiah in Chicago to the running of the bulls in Pamplona.

Other short travel takes that are popular with editors center around dealing with specific travel problems, such as coping with stolen passports or keeping a back seat full of children under control while driving cross-country. Most often these pieces combine information and the sort of advice found in procedural how-tos.

SCORING ON SPORTS SHORTS

The top-selling sports one-pagers focus on equipment or events. Equipment articles usually combine general information on the subject with specific step-by-step how-to advice, such as "How to Buy Running Shoes That Really Fit."

The event piece either centers on a specific sporting event, such as the Little League world championships, or is what I call the generic event piece. This article most often starts out with one to three paragraphs of general information—about marathons, for example—then goes on to tell about a handful of different events of the same type that will be held during a specific time period, in a certain area, or for a special group of people.

MINDING YOUR BUSINESS

Business topics encompass everything from computers to conglomerates. The most salable kinds of business briefs are those focusing on new products or on trends and techniques—ways of doing business that are gaining popularity or enabling business people or consumers to accomplish their goals.

The new-product pieces appear in almost every kind of magazine. New foods and new items for the kitchen are featured in publications aimed at people in the food and beverage industry, magazines for those associated with hotels and restaurants and in consumer publications such as *Bon Appetit*. Innovative products for heating or communication, beauty care or leisure could be salable topics for an even wider array of publications.

You'll find trends-and-techniques business articles most often in business publications, trade publications, airline in-flights and general-interest magazines. They also are appearing with greater frequency in women's magazines, especially those aimed at women in management or who own their own businesses.

TO YOUR (WRITING) HEALTH

Health-related subjects lend themselves amazingly well to short formats, and given the current level of health and fitness awareness, pieces on health-related themes may be just what the doctor ordered to perk up a sickly bank account.

The most popular kinds of health-related pieces tell of medical breakthroughs (especially new methods of treating or diagnosing disease), fitness and nutrition. These articles often require quotes from authorities in the health field to give them credibility.

Another one-pager that will make your wallet healthier is the health-related how-to. Although these pieces on occasion require an author (or co-author) with some sort of medical credentials, most of them need no more than an occasional quote from an expert. "How to Choose the Fitness Program That's Right for You," "Ten Steps to Healthier Eating Habits" and "Making Sure Your Family Gets Enough Fresh Air" are the sorts of articles any 30-Minute Writer who knows how to ask the right questions can write.

What are the "right" questions? They are questions that elicit answers that will make your articles informative, interesting and/or entertaining. How can you determine what these questions are? For starters, as you're preparing your list, ask yourself what you would like to know about your subject. The "Ten Steps to Healthier Eating Habits" idea, for example, would lend itself to questions such as "How do I know when I'm not eating right?"; "What can I do when my job demands that 50 percent of my meals involve entertaining clients?"; "What if I have severe allergies/food restrictions?"; "Doesn't food that's good for you get boring?"; and "How can I make radical changes in our diet without upsetting my family?"

Then imagine your readers, with all different kinds of lifestyles, occupations and interests. What information would be helpful to them? Discuss your subject with friends and co-work-ers. Find out what they would like to know about it.

In addition to asking your prepared questions, when you're at the interview, ask your interviewee for his or her view of the sub-ject in general. Then as the person speaks, jot down specific ques-tions about the various points made.

OLDIES BUT GOODIES

You'll notice that a great many pieces are written about subjects that—if you're old enough—you've seen time and time again. They're topics that never seem to grow stale since a new generation of readers is always coming along. Pieces on saving money at the supermarket, handling a difficult boss, adding closet space, and teaching your kids to tell the truth fall into this category. These articles are basically either project or problem-solving how-tos.

Obviously, if you're writing less than 1,000 words, the project/problem can't be too complex. But most of these "revolving door" topics don't need to be.

YOUR STYLE SHOWS

Whether you write one-pagers that tell readers how to do it or that make them feel informed, you have to do it in the style to which the magazine's editors are accustomed. When the word length is short, however, most magazines' patterns for success have a lot in common.

First of all, they're tightly written. Leads are short, generally only a few sentences. The "just-right" adjectives have to do what the writer needs them for—amplify the subject without wasting words. Quotes, when they're used, don't ramble. They're usually short and to the point. Anecdotes have to be brief, too, and often do double-duty as the lead or ending of the piece.

Whether the subject is about turning trash into home heat or organic baby food, information is transmitted best in short senten-ces and paragraphs. The reason is cosmetic as well as practical. A page filled with 40-word sentences and half-page paragraphs looks daunting to the person who wants a quick read.

FAST-BREAKING SALES

The easiest one-pager to write, to my way of thinking, is the newsbreak. It's considered the bread-and-butter piece by many freelancers, because for writers who can keep up production, it supplies a steady source of income.

Whereas many articles have a lifespan of several months (or even years), the newsbreak has an immediacy about it, a "this is the latest" slant. You'll find these timely news items in a host of publications, both general interest and specialized: trade publications, technological journals, and magazines about everything from fishing to antiques.

The basic classifications of newsbreaks, according to my system of keeping track, are *breakthrough/innovation*, *event*, *place* and *business briefs*. All of them are written in journalism's inverted-pyramid format, the form used for the majority of newspaper articles. The main point is presented in the lead paragraph (almost always in the first sentence), and succeeding points are given in order of importance.

Each point is generally amplified by a sentence or two of additional information (referred to as the *New York Times* style by editors). Paragraphs most often consist of two or three sentences — rarely more than four. The practical reasons for this style are that readers get the most important information in a hurry and editors can cut the article to fit available space at the end of any paragraph.

Style is crisp and reportorial, seldom employing devices such as similes, metaphors and anecdotes. This makes the newsbreak a natural for writers with newspaper experience, but it's an easy style for any writer to catch on to quickly.

The *breakthrough/innovation* category covers new developments (especially in science and medicine), new ways of doing things (big in the trade journals) and new products.

The *event* piece tells about a happening of interest to the magazine's readers, be it a church conclave, a dog show or a bowling tournament.

The *place* newsbreak is most often found in travel publications, primarily in the trades, such as *TravelageWest*, and travel bulletins, such as the *Travelore Report*. In travel trade publications, these pieces focus on news of vacation spots: hotels that are offering special rates, theme parks that are opening or expanding, sporting facilities that are adding new equipment (such as snow-making machines at ski resorts), and the like.

Business briefs report on everything from mergers to the employment picture to the fluctuations of the prime rate. You will encounter these bits of information from the financial world not only in business magazines, but also in publications like *Newsweek* and *Advertising Age*.

WHEN (AND IF) TO POP THE QUESTION

When writing articles of 1,000 words or more, my advice is to query whenever possible so that you won't have to expend effort writing articles that have little chance of selling. And although editors will almost always ask to see a completed personal essay or humorous article before committing to buy, it's a good idea to send a short query letter before submitting the finished piece. Anecdotes, hints, tips and the like are sent to editors in their completed form, without querying.

There isn't, however, one hard and fast rule when it comes to querying editors about one-page pieces. There are, instead, several hard and not-so-fast rules.

For example, any magazine listing in *Writer's Market* that specifies "no unsolicited manuscripts" will require a query, no matter what the length of the piece. But isn't it a bit silly to write a 300-word query about a 700-word piece? Therefore, you'll want to either send a brief letter of inquiry or try a short phone call.

If the article is dependent to a great degree on photos and contains a minimum of prose, chances are the editor will want to see the finished product, but again, you'll want to query before sending the piece.

Finally, if you feel that your short piece is one that could work in several magazines and that it's one you really want to write, go ahead. Your best chance of selling it will be to low-visibility magazines that accept unsolicited manuscripts, but newsstand publications are worth trying, too, if your idea's a really good one that fits.

In the case of newsbreaks—when time is of the essence—you can't afford the days it takes to query by mail. Either phone the editor or write the piece in its entirety and hope that you haven't been scooped.

Many beginning writers feel that phoning editors risks alienating them. I have found, to the contrary, that if my ideas are good ones and professionally presented—that is, concisely synopsizing the idea, its focus and my information resources—editors respond positively to telephone communication. Of course, if they like my ideas, they'll usually want a follow-up proposal in writing. But even if they can't use them, we've saved both the editor's time and mine.

RESEARCH MINUTE-SAVERS

Spending three days—or even three hours—finding facts for a twenty-five dollar piece doesn't make much sense when you don't need 90 percent of the information you've gathered. The "tip of the iceberg" theory—that what you write about a subject should be a small fraction of your total knowledge of it—is all well and good if you've the luxury of scads of time and money. But you'll save hours of research (and consequently have more time for writing articles) by reading similar articles in back issues of your intended publication. That way you can determine the sorts of questions you will want to answer in your piece.

It is not my intention here to tell you everything there is to know about research. Good books like *Writer's Essential Desk Reference* (Writer's Digest Books, 1991) and *Knowing Where to Look: The Ultimate Guide to Research* (Writer's Digest Books, 1988) will help you acquire the necessary skills.

But since effective research is vital to the 30-Minute Writer's economic survival, the following tips will help you get the most value out of the time you spend.

The answers you seek will in most cases be found through

interviews (personal, telephone and via letters), on-the-scene research, library research or a combination of these methods.

You'll need to do some detective work to locate authorities when your piece calls for quotes, statistics and opinions from experts. My starting point is usually the library's reference section. There I can find books containing lists of individuals in a given profession (lawyers or psychiatrists, for instance) and organizations such as the National Association of Manufacturers or the Future Farmers of America. These directories give addresses and phone numbers that will help you track down your experts. Don't neglect to consult *Books in Print* for the names of authors of books on your subject (write them in care of their publishers).

Suppose, for example, that you need views from three authorities on the relationship of soil selenium levels to the incidence of certain diseases. Your first step would be to look at *Subject Guide to Books in Print* under "Vitamins and Minerals." Next, you would seek out any directories of organizations dealing with nutrition. You would either call or write to those organizations that sound most promising to ask for names and addresses of experts in the field of selenium research. A half-hour of well-spent research time should in most cases yield a bumper crop of experts' names.

You will also often find experts named in articles that have been written on your subject (tracing them can be difficult, however, unless the articles mention their affiliations with organizations, universities and the like). Other expert-locating aid is available at colleges and universities. Simply phone the department related to your subject and ask for names of the kinds of authorities you need.

Before any interview, write down the questions you plan to ask. Make them specific and sharply focused on your subject. General, vague questions produce general, vague answers.

Don't let your interview paraphernalia slow you down. If you plan to use a tape recorder, know how to operate it and be sure the batteries are fresh. Have your prepared questions where you can find them immediately. If you plan to take notes, be sure that you have two or three functioning ballpoints or pencils.

To avoid confusion, at the outset of the interview tell the interviewee what the article will be about—even if you have given the same information over the phone when you made the appointment. You might add a phrase like, "Since it will be a rather short piece, I'm hoping to keep questions and answers as sharply focused as possible." That will alert your subject not to ramble.

PUTTING THEM TOGETHER

Winning one-pagers are usually written with strong active verbs and nouns. To be effective, writing has to be clear, crisp and concise. Adjectives and adverbs are used sparingly.

Summary leads and endings are most often used for the simple reason that they get to the point fast and exit quickly. In short travel pieces especially, the descriptive lead is also used.

When you begin writing, you'll save yourself rewriting grief if you abide by these rules:

1. Stick to the article's focus. With each sentence, ask yourself, Does this relate directly to my subject? Would the purpose of the piece suffer if I left it out?
2. Present your points in logical order. An article that goes directly from facet A to B to C requires fewer transitions.
3. Don't waste words telling readers what they already know. Avoid phrases like "Have you ever wondered . . . ?" and "You know, of course, that. . . ."
4. Delete unnecessary examples and anecdotes. One fact or little story (or two at most) will illustrate a point sufficiently.
5. Look for word wasters. Instead of writing "at the present time" say "now." "If" conveys the same meaning as "in the event of."
6. Cut the negative from any positive/negative portions of the piece. For example, "The solution is not in watering your plants every day. It lies in watering them when the soil feels dry" uses twenty words. "Water your plants when the soil feels dry" says the same thing with eight.

I've found, too, that fitting my material into the prescribed length is much easier if I make a rough outline after I've completed my research but before I begin writing. I read my research notes and put asterisks in the margins opposite the material I would like to include (three asterisks for the most important, two for that next in importance, and one for "if there's room" material). Then I write "lead" or "intro," followed by the number of points I would like to make and then the word "closing."

Next, I scan my notes for good lead material and write the approximate number of words I'll need to use opposite "lead." I try to use material I've marked with three asterisks in that lead, killing two space-takers with one stroke of the pen. Important information used in the lead won't have to go in the body of the piece, thus freeing more words for that part of the article. After "closing" I almost always write "100 words." It's the maximum number one can use to wind up a short piece. The writing job becomes easier if you can hone your closing shot to 50 words.

With a 100-word lead and 100-word closing allotment, 550 words are left for the body of a 750-word article. I've learned from experience that at least 100 words are usually needed to make a specific point, so I look at my asterisked notes to find the four or five most important facets of the subject. I begin writing when my outline looks something like this:

> Lead: 100 words—statistics on child abuse
> Point 1 and example: 150 words—outright mistreatment
> Point 2 and example: 150 words—negligence
> Point 3 and example: 100 words—thoughtlessness
> Point 4 and example: 150 words—what's being done to correct situation
> Closing: 100 words—sources of information on getting help for abusive parents

If, after writing according to this advice, your piece is still too long (one of the most common problems of beginning writers, especially, is overwriting), cutting it down need not be a teeth-gritting task. If your piece is more than 50 words too long, try to delete whole paragraphs. If the excess is less than 50, you'll probably be able to meet the limit by eliminating superfluous words and phrases rather than resorting to major cuts.

If you've gathered more facts than you need, you haven't wasted your time. Look at that information as input you've acquired for your personal knowledge bank—or use it to write another one-pager.

Like almost every other kind of work, writing short articles becomes easier after you have written a few. You will begin to know instinctively which kinds of information you need and what you can leave out. You'll become adept at telling the story simply and clearly—the essence of true communication.

THE 30-MINUTE WRITER'S PLAN OF ACTION

1. Become familiar with at least a dozen one-pager markets that you feel you might write successfully for.

2. Start generating ideas. When you think of a viable topic, write it down. Unpenned ideas have a way of escaping from our busy minds.

3. Do basic research. Don't spend more time than you need to determine whether the article idea is a viable one.

4. Decide whether you need to query the editor before writing your piece. A good rule of thumb here—in addition to those stated earlier in the chapter—is to balance the estimated time composing a query would take against the estimated time needed to write the piece.

5. Start writing. Be sure that the piece is sharply focused, that the theme is developed without the inclusion of extraneous material. Make sure your sentences are predominantly declarative (in case you've forgotten, a declarative sentence is one that makes a statement) and that the quotes you use are short, concise and contribute information on your subject.

6. Do a professional job of presenting your work. Copy

should be clean, without typos. Your name, address, telephone and Social Security number should be single-spaced at the top of the first page of the manuscript. The title and text (double-spaced) should begin one-third of the way down the page. The left-hand margin should be about an inch, and the right hand margin a half-inch wider. Identify succeeding pages with a slug (one or two words of the article's title) and the page number before you proceed with the text.

7. Keep your piece in circulation. If it doesn't work for the first editor, send it to the next one on your list. Persistent writers finally sell almost all of their pieces — if they're well written.

CHAPTER IV

The Not-So-Well-Developed Personality

Now, I'll be the first one to admit that it takes years to get to know most people really well. But I'll also be the first to argue that in half an hour, you can get to know a person well enough—at least on one dimension—to write a 300- to 900-word personality piece.

Add the handful of half hours it takes for market research, the couple more to decide what person to interview, three or four to write the piece and you have a perfect 30-Minute Writer project.

It's made more perfect by the fact that people pieces are among the most popular with editors of most publications. They provide the human interest element so essential to reader satisfaction.

These cameos are among the most interesting and lucrative minis to write. Interviews are as exciting as those for longer personality pieces but less demanding, since they don't require as much time or as many questions. And you can get twice the information you'll ever need in that half-hour interview by writing out twenty-five to thirty questions in advance.

Unless you're writing about a celebrity or public figure, there probably won't be any material on your subject at the library. At most, you'll need just a few minutes to check (be sure to glance through city/state/regional publications and newspaper clipping files if there's a chance your personality has been written about in local publications).

As for other research, since the miniprofiles are usually not multidimensional, you won't have to interview anyone other than your subject. Then too, you can use the leftovers from full-length profile interviews to write shorter personality pieces about the same people for different publications. Seasoned pros deliberately ask a few "extra" questions at each interview. The responses provide material that they can use for other pieces — either about the same subject or as part of an article about several people with something in common.

Best of all, the central figures in abbreviated personality pieces don't have to be headline entertainers or Nobel Prize winners. They don't even have to be as "slightly famous" as the winner of the International Whistle-Off.

The only requirement for minipersonality subjects is that they have to be people who do or have done something just a bit out of the ordinary. You'll find these people in cities and hamlets all over the world.

What this means to you, the writer, is that you can craft minipersonalities about people who are readily accessible. And that's a real time-saver. While it is often difficult to obtain interviews with celebrities (Martin Agronsky, the story goes, persevered four years before getting a television interview with former Justice Hugo L. Black of the U.S. Supreme Court), most noncelebrities are flattered by the idea that they're considered interesting enough to be the subjects of articles.

In time, as your skills expand and credits pile up, you may find yourself interviewing the world's famous. But for starters, you've a better shot at interviewing the not-so-well-knowns.

Chances are, you won't have to spend a lot of time traveling to your interviews either. As I said, every community, no matter how small, has its share of people worth writing about. The only problem in identifying these people is that you're often so close that you take them for granted, without thinking of the attributes that make them special.

The 75-year-old widow down the street who has turned her home into a hospice for AIDS victims; the high school student who's well on the way to becoming a millionaire by mass producing the low-cost widget he invented; the member of the board of a failed savings and loan who is working to regain respect—people like these are the raw material used by successful writers to craft their profiles.

PERSONALITY MODIFICATION

Just as potential subjects have individual characteristics, so do the magazines to which you must match them. Although the longer, fully developed profiles in *Parade* and other broad readership publications approach their subjects from all angles—background, business, families, friends and enemies, homelife, hobbies, recreational pursuits, past triumphs and future plans—there just isn't space in the miniprofile for all that.

You'll find, therefore, that the miniprofile is sharply focused, usually with a single angle directly related to the purpose of the magazine in which it appears. Some tie-ins are obvious. Others are less apparent. But everything you need to know about targeting your profile material can be learned by reading a few issues of the publications you think might accept your ideas.

The only requirement for profile subjects in *Woman*, for instance, is that they are females doing things that will be of interest to other women. Presented in a department called "Women in the News," these very short profiles feature such people as Pam Erickson, founder of an organization called Professional Respite Care, which gives relief to families caring for ill or elderly relatives, and Julie Brice, the young president of the ICBIY chain of frozen yogurt stores, but they also tell about homemakers whose endeavors and accomplishments are somehow special.

Miniprofiles in *Entrepreneurial Woman*, by contrast, always deal with women in business. They focus on the way the subject got into her business, how she financed it, what techniques she has used to attract customers and deal with different aspects of the business—innovative financing and merchandising, efficient delivery of products, methods of finding and dealing with manufacturers.

Country Woman's profiles have titles like "Whoa! Modern-Day

Western Wagon Master Is . . . A Mrs!" and "Country Wife's Comments Make Powerful Horse Sense." The former is about the woman who led Idaho's centennial wagon train. The latter spotlights a Kansas woman whose goal is to announce the national horse-pulling championships.

Profiled personalities in magazines for seniors like *Golden Years* and *New Choices for the Best Years* are always over the age of fifty, usually older. Popular themes are second careers, overcoming the problems of retirement, keeping young, athletic achievements, helping others and unusual activities. If the magazine is sponsored by a particular religious denomination or an association of retired people who were formerly involved in the same occupation, the profile subjects will, in addition, usually be members of the same denomination or retirement organization.

Profiles in *Mpls.-St. Paul*, on the other hand, don't have to be of business owners or franchisees, or about people in a particular age group. But the subjects do have to be involved in the Twin Cities area, whether as street entertainer or symphony orchestra concertmaster.

And as with any regional magazine, you'll need to find a sharp focus. It might be that the world-class athlete attributes her success to readily accessible training facilities in the Twin Cities area or that the artist gets his inspiration from watching the wildlife around his Minnesota lake home. But whatever angle you choose, there must be a focus beyond the fact that your subject is a local.

VIP MINIS AND MINI-VIPS

So far we have talked primarily about not-so-prominent people as your profile subjects since they usually are more time-efficient as far as the 30-Minute Writer is concerned. But some of you may have access to the rich and famous, perfect for the mini-celebrity profile. Maybe you live next door to the star quarterback for an NFL team. Perhaps your sister is the executive secretary at a leading L.A. talent agency. She knows top entertainers and TV stars on a first-name basis and is certain they would talk to you because her boss okayed the idea. If that's the case, by all means go for it.

Real life usually doesn't work that way, however. Most stars are very busy people. They—and their agents—usually welcome publicity but aren't too obliging unless the writer who wants an interview has a firm assignment from a publication the star or agent feels is important. But there are exceptions. A former writing student of mine, for example, was able to interview Red Skelton (she reported he was charming) without an assignment.

The question is, therefore, do you approach the celebrity's agent before you have the assignment, hoping you'll be granted an interview? Or do you write the editor of your targeted magazine a query before you have the interview nailed down? It's embarrassing (and alienating) if you get the editor's go-ahead and then can't obtain the interview. Since I would rather be turned down by a celebrity's agent than alienate an editor, the former course seems the wiser.

Unless you and the celebrity buy your toothpaste at the same drugstore and have established some kind of "How are you today?" relationship, you'll most likely have to contact his or her agent to try to get an interview. You can find out who that agent is by getting in touch with the TV studio that produces his sitcoms, the club where she frequently performs, the record company that puts out his albums or her publisher.

Approaching an agent can be scary. Some of them are incredibly rude; others, nice as pie. Be up-front in your approach. Say that you don't have a firm assignment but that you're confident you can place the piece. Either mail or hand deliver clips of your published work if you have any.

An alternative, of course, is to lay your cards on the table during your first contact with the editor. Propose the article you plan to write, then say something like "I am quite sure that I will be able to obtain the necessary interview, but want you to understand that I cannot get _____'s agent to commit until I have a firm assignment."

There may be times when you have access to a child celebrity without benefit of agent, if say, his grandmother lives around the corner from you or her little sister attends your child's preschool.

The temptation to write the piece after talking off-the-cuff with the kid who has made two hundred commercials or is ranked as the country's number one junior tennis player may be great. Restrain yourself from writing, however, until you've spoken to the child's parents or whoever else is legally in charge. Although adult celebrities, as public figures, are fair game unless it can be proved they were libeled, the courts look more protectively upon children, famous or not.

PERSONALITY TYPES

Not only are the kinds of people you'll write about determined by the focus of a publication, the point of view, style, breadth of focus and length should be influenced by your targeted magazine as well.

By and large, miniprofiles are written from a sympathetic point of view. For one thing, it's difficult to write an evenhanded controversial piece in 900 words or less. Short profiles are usually written from the human interest aspect, playing to readers' curiosities, but the extent to which personal information is divulged varies greatly from publication to publication.

Writing styles range from no-nonsense reportorial to chatty. The skilled miniprofiler uses style to project the subject's personality. If her conversation is breezy, a couple of quippy quotes will tell the reader more than a long descriptive passage could. Adjectives, chosen precisely, can further add flesh and blood to the portrait. If she sits informally, with her legs tucked under her skirt or if he twists the corner of his tie before he answers a question, get that into the piece.

And make each quote count. Rather than going into a lengthy explanation of how the subject feels about going from a pro-life job to becoming a pro-choice volunteer, for example, you might use a quote like this: "I don't know what was most repugnant to me about the job," she says, munching on her thumbnail, "counseling a pregnant woman against abortion or watching her give her baby up for adoption."

As for breadth of focus, one magazine may want a once-over

light survey of the subject's life and career, another may shun anything other than information that relates directly to the subject's battle against multiple sclerosis. The subject's age is almost always mentioned, but you can't take that as a given. And although marital status figured in the profiles of a decade ago, now you'll usually find only a passing reference or none at all. In the case of profiles of women in business, you will rarely see the "her husband is so supportive" prose of yesteryear.

Generally, minis fall into three size formats. Most popular seem to be those that, along with a picture, fill one page and run about 800 to 900 words. Half-pagers run 300 to 400 words, and the length of two-column pieces falls somewhere between the full- and half-page lengths.

Occasionally, you'll find even shorter profiles, like those in *Midwest Living*. The subjects usually are people who live in midwestern states who produce out-of-the-ordinary objects, like Hmong refugee Khang Yang who lives in a Twin Cities suburb and creates exquisite embroidered pillowcases. Other subjects have included a potter whose specialty figurines are called "Winkles." No matter what their length, miniprofiles almost always include a photo of the featured person.

Some magazines will expect you to provide pictures of the personality. On occasion, the interviewee will be able to supply them (show business people's agents, especially, seem to have stacks of black-and-white glossies and color slides of their clients), but most of the time the job will be up to you. If you don't feel that your photographic abilities measure up to the magazine's standards, make a deal with a freelance photographer. Decide what kinds of shots you'll need by studying the photos accompanying the magazine's previously published profiles.

Another magazine that uses personality pieces of the 180-230 word variety is *Los Angeles Magazine*. To illustrate how much information can be conveyed in a few words by a skillful writer, here's a mini-mini titled "Victoria Brynner: The King and Her" written for the magazine by Deborah Sroloff.

Looking at her you'd think she'd spend most of her time in front of the camera. But as a world-class photojournalist and director of operations for the popular Italian magazines *King* and *Moda*, Brynner actually does her best work behind it.

As it turns out, actor Yul Brynner's only daughter did begin as a model. "I signed with Elite and moved to Paris when I was 20," says Brynner, now 28, who was born and raised in Switzerland and now lives in L.A. "But I was uncomfortable. While I liked the attention, I wanted something more lasting."

She inherited her fascination with photography from her father, once a lensman with Robert Capa's legendary Magnum Agency. She began by taking head shots of her model friends for their portfolios; not long after, she landed an exclusive to shoot former Pakistani prime minister Benazir Bhutto with her newborn daughter—and she's gone on to photograph the late shah of Iran's son for *People*, as well as such family friends as Elizabeth Taylor, Audrey Hepburn and Julio Iglesias.

But having an insider's edge doesn't necessarily make things any easier. "The better you know people," Brynner laughs, "the harder it can be to photograph them."

It's not difficult to figure out why this miniprofile sold. First of all, the subject isn't just any accomplished photojournalist; she's also Yul Brynner's daughter. And since just about everybody is interested in movie stars'/celebrities' kids, that hooks the reader right away.

The lead—two great sentences—is another of the piece's many strengths. The two quotes tell a lot about the subject. The remaining sentences tell a good deal about her career. And notice the neat transitional sentence starting off the final paragraph. The article's only weakness is that we would like to know more about the subject—and that's perhaps a strength in itself.

INTERVIEWING INSIGHTS

The interviewing tips for one-pagers (see chapter three) apply to miniprofiles as well. An additional technique, which has worked well for me, is to begin the interview by complimenting the interviewee on some item of his or her apparel—an unusual pin, a splashy tie—or, if we are in the person's home, on an interesting decorating accessory such as a hand-carved table.

This sort of conversation usually does two things. It relaxes the interviewee, and responses like "Oh, I bought it at a flea market or at a souk in Mecca or at Niemann Marcus" give the interviewer additional insights into the person he or she is interviewing.

Sharp interviewers have other tricks to make every minute of the short interview count. Celia Scully, who has interviewed authorities ranging from bioethicists to airline presidents, says "When I've only got a few minutes with a VIP, I'm forced to reverse my usual procedure of building up to the tough questions. I've found that if I wait, the interviewee may signal 'time's up' before I've gotten answers I want most."

It is never a good idea to ask questions that can be answered with a simple "Yes" or "No" unless your next question will be "Why?" And do your best to be nonconfrontational, no matter how you feel about a subject. Remember: You're a reporter, not judge and jury.

Asking the tough question is the hardest part of any interview. Good technique demands that you establish a nonadversarial rapport with the person you're interviewing, but it's difficult to appear nonconfrontational when you're asking questions that touch a raw spot in his psyche, that imply she's doing a bad job or has no sense of aesthetics. Use phrases like "It's been alleged that . . ." or "Your critics say that . . . " or "What do you think caused the problem of. . . ."

Most interviewees will respond positively to a friendly, nonthreatening approach. If you can get across the idea that you're fair-minded while you move your subject onto the difficult topic, you'll be able to ask hard questions without antagonizing anyone.

Good interviewers agree that it's a plus if you can interview your subject in his or her natural habitat—home, office or place of business. Try to arrive a bit early so that you can concentrate on the atmosphere and make notes on the surroundings.

There's another benefit to the early arrival. Since you're a 30-Minute Writer, you're most likely no stranger to split-second timing. If you arrive out of breath and worried about being late, your subject won't be at ease either. And during the interview, don't get so preoccupied with the ticking clock that you're unable to do your job effectively.

Speaking of celebrity interviews, every once in a while you'll run into an agent who insists on answering questions even though you pointedly direct them at the celebrity. If this sort of behavior persists, calmly turn to the agent and say in firm tones that you would like to hear the responses directly from his/her client.

Keeping on track and under control can be a problem no matter who you're interviewing. Some people tend to ramble. Others overexplain. Both when you make the appointment and at the outset of the interview, say something like "I'm only going to take half an hour of your time and I have quite a number of questions to ask you about things that will interest my readers." Then, when a difficult interview starts disintegrating into digressions and irrelevancies, you can bring it back with a gentle, "That's very interesting and I'd love to hear about it another time, but. . . ." Then ask your next question. If you're too polite, however, you may end up without enough information to write your piece.

IT'S YOUR LEAD

As with any short article, your lead can mean the difference between a winning article and one that goes down to defeat in the rejects pile. Currently, the three most popular leads as far as editors are concerned are summary, quote and descriptive.

The summary can get you into your subject without using more than a sentence or two: Take this one from *Entrepreneurial Woman* called "All the Right Moves." You can see that its construction is straightforward—no wasting words on fancy writing:

> For Betsy Collins, moving to a new city after a divorce turned into a profitable venture.

With only sixteen words, author Frances Huffman set the stage to tell about the woman's success in establishing a business that welcomes newcomers to the community.

The quote lead, using an appropriate statement, by either the featured person or one of his or her associates, also is a favorite curtain-raiser for the miniprofile. This one appeared in *Woman's Day* in a very short piece called "Dick Clark's MVP":

"Given a choice between extremely busy or extremely bored, I'd choose busy," says Kari Clark, vice president of administration for dick clark productions.

Whether or not they begin with quotes, most miniprofiles contain a large proportion of direct quotations. Allowing people to tell about their work or hobbies or adventures in their own words gives readers not only information but also insight into their personalities. In the article about Kari Clark, for instance, 112 of the 232 words in the piece were directly quoted.

There's no "good" ratio of words in quotation marks to total number of words in the piece. To determine how many quotes you'll need for articles you write, examine the minis your targeted editor has chosen in the past and count the number of quotes and words in each of them. Some articles may seem heavy on quotes to you; others may seem light. But what the editor wants, the editor should get.

Since it's a rare personality piece that doesn't call for at least two or three quotes, this can present real problems when your subject is a mumbler or answers in monosyllables. People who do interesting things aren't necessarily interesting to talk to. When you've failed to coax scintillating sayings from your subject's lips despite your best efforts, don't despair. Talk to his friends, her business associates, the family priest, and quote their comments. It may take longer than you had planned, but at least you'll get something to write about.

Although the descriptive lead is the least-often used of the three most popular miniprofile leads, it can be extremely effective in giving readers a feel for the subject's personality or his surroundings. This one is from "Mirella Ricciardi" by Daniel Butler in *Mirabella*:

> A pair of buffalo horns hangs above Mirella Ricciardi's front door, bleaching in the polluted city rain. She said I'd recognize the house and she was right. The horns are an appropriate symbol for a photographer raised in the Kenyan bush, if a little incongruous for fashionably rundown inner London.
>
> Inside, cushions are strewn across the floor, and plants cascade along the walls. Wicker and pine dominate the furnishings. A conservatory looks onto a small courtyard. The doors are open in spite of the drizzle.
>
> Footsteps clatter down the stairs and Mirella Ricciardi bursts into the room. Sixty years spent mainly outdoors is not supposed to be good for the complexion, but the exposure hasn't harmed hers. She is lithe, tanned and striking, dressed cossack-style in a black sweater and light-cotton culottes tucked into leather boots. Casting a photographer's eye over me, she fires a barrage of questions in a husky Italian accent. Suddenly she relaxes and sits back. The test is over, the impatience disappears, and for the next two and a half hours she holds me enthralled.

That lead is an uncommonly long one for a short profile (almost one third of the piece), but see how much information about the person it conveys?

A fourth lead, the anecdote, while popular for longer personality pieces, is difficult to incorporate into the shorter piece, since most anecdotes require a disproportionately large number of words to tell the little stories.

WHOSE LEAD SHOULD YOU FOLLOW?

To determine which of these leads to use, consider the editor's past preferences. Some editors favor summary leads; others consistently buy pieces that begin with quotes. Try to fashion your lead after those your editor prefers. But keep your material and subject in mind, too.

The information gleaned from some interviews simply doesn't lend itself to certain kinds of leads. If you have to interview your subject in a bare and blah-looking room and he answers your questions soberly and directly without smiling or exhibiting any distinguishing mannerisms, you won't have much material to write a descriptive lead. On the other hand, your subject may greet you in her pink satin boudoir, wearing an orange antebellum gown and fifteen pieces of jewelry, surrounded by her pet chimp and three talking birds.

BREATHING LIFE INTO THE BODY

However you lead into your article, you must from the beginning do everything you can to let readers know what makes your archeologist or dogsled maker or Supreme Court justice tick. Is he short or tall? Does she speak like a nuclear physicist or with down-home simplicity? How does he feel about traditional family life? What are her views on keeping pets in apartments? A peek at a personality, however fleeting, must reveal a three-dimensional, flesh-and-blood character.

As you read miniprofiles, be aware of why you do or do not enjoy reading them. Chances are, those that don't interest you are just characteristics on paper instead of human beings to whom you can relate.

As an exercise, read a number of profiles and make lists of questions that would elicit the articles' information. When you begin doing interviews, you'll be able to modify these lists to form nuclei for your own questions.

LAST GLIMPSES

Don't concentrate so much on ending your miniprofile that you forget that the words you use must provide information as well as wrap up the piece. The quote ending is the one you'll find most often—perhaps because it's such a great vehicle for giving last-minute insights into the subject. While they're interviewing their subjects, the pros look for appropriate end quotes and make some sort of notation to indicate those that are possibilities.

Ending the miniprofile is not so difficult, either, if you keep the purpose of your piece in mind. Whatever facet of your subject the article focuses on should be reiterated or reinforced in those final sentences.

If the piece points up your subject's sunny nature in the face of adversity, close with a quote from your interview that illustrates the person's marvelous sense of humor. When your article focuses on the subject's athletic prowess, you might want to close with a summary (the second most popular miniprofile ending) about her past accomplishments or goals for the future.

Almost all of the structural requirements of miniprofiles work for full-blown pieces as well. There's just one difference. Because of the stringent length limitations in the short pieces, you have to craft them so that every single word has a purpose and does its job better than any other word can.

PERSONALITY PICTURES

Although some magazines prefer to have an assigned photographer take pictures on their behalf, you'll often be called upon to provide photos of your personality. Pay close attention to the kinds of pictures the publication you're writing for has printed in the past. Like the words, those photos will give you the clues to your success.

The trend generally, especially in the case of noncelebrities, is to have one to three photos accompany the miniprofile. Usually, they're taken in the context of the subject's activities — teaching children with cerebral palsy to swim, picnicking with the family, building birdhouses. And though there may be other people in the photos, the subject is always featured, i.e., you won't have to spend a lot of time figuring out who he or she is. The pictures' primary function is to give readers more information, satisfying their curiosity as to what the subject looks like.

Although we can mentally picture many celebrities when we read their names, photos accompanying miniprofiles about them aren't merely art. If people are interested enough in a celebrity to read an article about him or her, they will enjoy looking at pictures, too—especially if they aren't the same Princess Di shots they've seen ever since 1981.

Even though celebrity head shots and pictures of stars with their children and/or significant others are still popular in publications such as *Parade*, there's a swing toward showing celebrities in more candid settings.

The photos accompanying the miniprofiles in *New Choices*, for instance, feature celebrities in the environments most of us would identify them with—like Julia Child in the kitchen or former senator Barry Goldwater in the amateur radio room of his home, with a typically Arizona backdrop visible through the windows. And since it has become fashionable for stars to become activists, you're likely to see pictures of TV heroines recycling trash and basketball stars shooting baskets with members of boys' clubs.

A number of magazines, operating on the "picture worth a thousand words" principle, like to use multiple photos with each miniprofile. *Country Woman* uses as many as five. If you have to furnish the pictures, send as many good ones (ten to twenty, if possible) as you can. As mentioned earlier, the interviewee can sometimes supply them.

If not, and you don't feel that your photographic ability measures up to the magazine's standards, make a deal with a freelance photographer. When the magazine pays separately for photos, you can agree to pay that amount to the photographer. If payment is made for the text/photo package, arrange to pay her a percentage of the total amount. Even if photos aren't required by the editor, snap a few, if you can, to refer to while you're writing the piece. It's amazing how many details you will recall simply by looking at the pictures.

THE WRITE CHOICE

I hope that while you've been reading the examples in this chapter, you have been reminded of interesting people you might feature in miniprofiles of your own. They are everywhere—appearing in town on the lecture circuit or sitting on the front porch two houses down. Look for people in unlikely professions or with unusual hobbies. People who have conquered adversity are naturals for the tabloids and women's magazines. For example, more than a half-dozen articles have been written about Grace Layton Sandness, many of them appearing in major publications.

Grace, who was felled by polio at age nineteen and is paralyzed from the neck down, has lived her past forty-two years in a wheelchair. Nonetheless, this courageous woman and her husband took twelve children—several of them handicapped—into their hearts and home.

Grace can't move her arms or legs, and she operates her wheelchair by blowing through a tube that controls the motor. A respirator that fits across her chest keeps her breathing.

Her brood of foster and adopted children include four Americans, four Koreans, three Ehtiopians and one Vietnamese. Aesoon had heart surgery. Kim had severe emotional problems. Cindy has cerebral palsy; Jennifer had polio. Three others have handicaps, too. But since Grace and her children have their handicaps in common. She has been able to help them in ways that a normal mother couldn't.

Despite Grace's handicap, she and her husband Dave have also founded an adoption agency. And since 1976, she's placed hundreds of homeless children from around the world with loving families. She has also written two books, typing out the words with a plastic stick clenched between her teeth.

I chose to tell you about this profile personality because the story emphasizes a most important point: The best subjects for personality pieces are often too close for us to see them. I should have written that piece. As a child, I walked to school with Grace. We went to the same Sunday school. Though my family moved from the town where both Gracie and I grew up, I knew about her tragedy and subsequent triumphs.

Every one of you has courageous, interesting, daring, inventive, inspiring, famous exciting people in your life. Don't pass them by.

THE 30-MINUTE WRITER'S PLAN OF ACTION

1. Browse through as many magazines as you can find, looking for those that use miniprofiles. Decide which of these magazines you'd like to write for and put them in a pile.

2. Head each of several sheets of paper with the name of one of the magazines in the pile. Add information on the average length of its miniprofiles and number of quotes. Write down phrases that describe the subjects of the magazines' profiles, for example, businesswoman, Roman Catholic, fifty-plus years old, retiree, celebrity, single parent, unusual occupation, rags to riches.

3. Think of interesting people in your area who have the characteristics on your lists and put their names on the appropriate pages. Choose the one that seems like your best subject for a successful piece.

4. Make an interview appointment and formulate twenty-five to thirty questions, based upon the kinds of answers previously published pieces contain.

5. If you didn't use a tape recorder, transcribe your notes as soon as possible after the interview. Add any information you remember but didn't have time to write down.

6. Write a brief outline of your piece. It need not be any more elaborate than this:

    A. Intro, including quote and sentence that points up focus of profile—85 to 95 words

    B. Two or three short examples that amplify/illustrate focus (include another quote, if possible)—300 words

    C. Closing (Use a quote if one not used above)—75 words

7. Write the piece, using your outline as a guide. Then polish it until every word fits your featured personality.

CHAPTER V

Sounding Off

ATTENTION: FORMER HIGH SCHOOL NEWSPAPER EDITORS

If those crusader fires still flame within you (or even just flicker a little), and if you have a spare thirty minutes now and then, there's a place for you in the writing world—even though you long ago gave up the dream of being London correspondent for the *New York Times*.

You might want to try your word processor at writing op-eds, those opinionated pieces that appear on the editorial pages of newspapers throughout the country and in regular departments of a variety of magazines.

Two decades ago, editorials were the province of editors. Period. Then, publications like the *Times* and *Newsweek* decided to inaugurate op-ed departments—opinions written in editorial form that would be chosen from reader submissions. More and more newspapers and magazines got in on the trend.

Following suit, some of the TV and radio stations included in their programming commentaries on current affairs by people other than their staffers. However, TV and radio opinion pieces don't seem to have generated the audiences that print media have.

As early as the mid-1970s, top writers were vying to appear on the op-ed pages of the more prestigious magazines. One freelancer

I know, who was earning enough to support his family handsomely, was delighted when his one-page op-ed was chosen by *Newsweek* for the "My Turn" department. "They're only paying me $500 — far less than what I usually get," he told us, "but the exposure's terrific."

Competition in the leading newspapers and magazines is still tough, but with the expanded market there are all levels of publications to which to submit. A quick look through *Writer's Market* shows that publications running the editorial gamut from *Artilleryman* to *Conceive Magazine, The Magazine of Infertility Issues*, use opinion pieces. Curiously, you'll rarely find requests for op-eds in the "Politics and World Affairs" section.

Several women's magazines print them, though, focusing on subjects geared to the audiences those magazines seek to attract. As you might imagine, the op-ed pieces in *Family Circle*'s "Full Circle" department are calculated to have broad reader interest, with titles such as "The Beauty Trap" and "Boys Will Be Boys?" The contention of the first piece is "Beauty is finding a way to enjoy all the things we are, without ignoring or distorting any part." The second decries the treatment of reporter Lisa Olson, who was humiliated by New England Patriot team members in a widely publicized locker-room incident.

Women's magazines with more targeted audiences, such as working women and women who are especially interested in fitness, might print op-eds with similar premises to those in *Family Circle*, but chances are they'll be aimed more specifically toward the topics that prompt their readers to buy the magazine.

About two dozen regional magazines specify opinion pieces among the kinds of nonfiction they're looking for, which is not surprising, since every part of the country is involved in controversy of some sort or other most of the time. But you'll also find requests for op-eds from markets you might not expect would use them, such as hobbies, crafts and gardening magazines. An opinion piece in one of the gardening magazines a couple of years ago actually drew so much flak that its editor expected a lawsuit.

Op-eds in *Newsweek*'s "My Turn" (payment is a thousand dollars now) deal with everything from getting rid of the Scrooge in all of us to a letter to Yasir Arafat; from the obsession with getting a good parking spot to teenage brutality and the legitimization of violence.

WHAT'S AN OP-ED?

Fully defining the op-ed isn't as simple as it may seem. Many of the opinion pieces you find in newspapers mirror the editorials written by those publications' staff in tone, style and content. They may, however, differ as far as point of view is concerned. Liberal pieces find their way to the op-ed pages of some newspapers with conservative leanings and vice versa.

Content, style, tone and point of view, however, aren't always those that we traditionally associate with the editorial format. This is especially true in the case of magazine op-ed departments.

Many of the differences reflect changes in society. Content has been affected by changing mores and interests as well as national and world events.

Tone is less formal than in the past, imitating a less formal social structure—one that has spawned, for example, the practice of addressing people we don't know by their first names in phone calls and correspondence.

Some op-eds are definitely conversational, complete with contractions and contemporary slang. Writers of even the most serious pieces have abandoned the rigid, preaching tone so popular in editorials of the past.

Point of view has become less self-censored. Twenty years ago, most people would have shied away from writing an opinion piece about such subjects as homosexuality or abortion even if they had strong convictions. But the Vietnam conflict, in addition to making us more cynical, convinced us that it was okay to speak out on issues.

It's also become more socially acceptable to entertain points of view that only a few decades ago would have been considered amoral, antisocial or heretical. And though the point of view taken in articles published by most magazines remains more traditional/

conventional, op-eds are the perfect foil for less widely held viewpoints.

This societal evolution, combined with the specialized magazine phenomenon, has resulted in the publication of op-eds on every topic from global warming and sexual harassment to going gray and compact discs. Just about anything goes if the topic is in sync with the publication—in sports magazines on sports; in women's magazines on subjects that pertain to the kind of women the magazine sees as its readers—and the piece approaches that subject in compatible tone and style.

The basic differences between the op-ed and personal essay (we'll discuss them in chapter ten) are that 1.) the subject of the former must in some way be controversial, and 2.) it must contain the clearly stated opinion of the writer, with the primary purpose being to influence the reader.

The op-ed is a sort of "listen to this side of the story" piece. Its writer is a messenger with a mission. His or her point of view is accompanied by evidence set forth in an attempt to give validity to the opinion.

Although the personal essay is often written completely in first person, the op-ed usually employs first person only in the opening paragraph or two—if at all. However, an important component of the piece is that even if words like "I believe" or "To my way of thinking" aren't used, they are implied. Subject matter—although it might well be the same for the op-ed as for the personal essay—is given a somewhat different treatment. Whereas in the latter it is looked at from a personal perspective, often with anecdotes involving the writer, the op-ed deals with the material in a more "opinionated" way.

For example, whereas the personal essay writer on drug-ridden neighborhoods might simply tell the story of how growing up in such an area affected her life, the writer of an op-ed on the same subject must set forth his opinion on the subject—why such neighborhoods exist, what in his opinion can be done to get rid of them, why they can't be eliminated, or his opinion on any other facet of his subject.

No wonder, then, that the line between the op-ed and personal essay is often blurred. Some magazines refer to material that is technically in the personal essay genre as op-ed. When they do, the wise writer either writes with an eye to the kind of content and style the editor has used in the past, or abandons those markets to find others that use true op-eds.

SOME OPINIONS ON BASICS

Newspaper op-eds remain the most traditionally editorial in style. However, the majority of magazine op-eds are similar in format. Typically, they set forth a problem or situation that exists—usually with anecdote or narrative—then go on to 1.) set forth the writer's perceptions as to why the problem/situation has come into being, and/or 2.) offer the writer's views on possible solutions.

In most op-eds, the writer advances three or four points to bolster his or her opinion. Each of these points may be illustrated anecdotally, with statistics and/or with quotes from authorities/ experts. The final paragraph or two contain the admonition that something must be done to solve the problem or alter the situation.

The following excerpts from a *Redbook Magazine* p.o.v. (point of view) opinion piece offer good examples of typical op-ed technique, although the p.o.v. department pieces in most issues are more often of the personal essay variety. The piece is called "The Feminist Mistake" and was written by Margaret Carlson. It begins:

> What do female newscasters, female soldiers and battered women have in common? The vanguard of the women's movement insists that they're all getting a raw deal.
>
> But instead, feminists may be missing the point. These activists may actually be doing women a disservice by carrying the equality banner to the far side of logic.

In the next 472 words, Carlson sets forth three supporting arguments against trying to force a one-size-fits-all equality onto every woman's life—one involving a TV newswoman, the second about mothers in the military, and the third about women murdering their husbands. Then she closes with this paragraph:

> The war for equality has not been won yet, but some of the battles have. It does not undercut the larger goals of feminism to know when to draw the line. Feminists must learn to resist the temptation to take a worthy cause too far. Imagine the backlash if women started getting away with murder.

Most op-ed pieces are about 1,000 words long. In magazines, the one-page pieces are often accompanied by a small drawing or picture — sometimes that of the author. In newspapers, they're almost always unadorned by art. Unlike personality pieces, articles on travel, sports and the outdoors, how-tos and most other articles, the op-ed's message is carried by words alone.

What does that mean to the writer who reads between the lines? First of all, that whatever the subject matter, op-eds are not meant to be frivolous. They're to be taken seriously. Secondly, that the readers who won't be intimidated by big blocks of type are looking for more "meat and potatoes" information than those who shy away from text without pictures. They're expecting to be stimulated by the controversy and, hopefully, to learn something in the process.

Even if the tone is light, the message is not meant to be taken lightly. Take the beginning of this piece called "Nine Brides for One Brother" in *Mademoiselle*'s "The Private Eye," a regular department written by Barbara Grizzuti Harrison:

> Oh, dear. Guess who's proselytizing now? On *Donahue* and in op-ed pieces in my hometown paper, the *New York Times*, and all over the place. Polygamists. They want some respect. They want to enjoy the privileged legal status of conventionally married persons; they want to be free to do all kinds of stuff conventionally married persons do, like adopt kids (in which hare-brained endeavor they have enlisted the American Civil Liberties Union, who you'd think might have better things to do with the money I send them). Most

of all, they want you to know that they have—while the rest of us limp along bewilderedly—snappily solved a compelling social problem of our time; juggling the conflicting demands of marriage, career and motherhood.

OP-ED IDEAS

Ideas for op-eds come from current events and just about every aspect of contemporary life. Skim a single issue of *USA Today* and you'll probably come up with a couple dozen ideas. Scan a financial publication or magazine devoted to health and you'll find a dozen more.

One of the best ways to get ideas is by reading op-eds published in as many different publications as you can find, because for most writers, reading stimulates creativity.

At times, you'll disagree violently with the author and start developing a rationale in support of an opposite view. Or you may agree with the writer's premise but for completely different reasons. Your associative mechanism may be primed, and a piece on victim's rights will trigger thoughts on the rights that you believe laid-off workers should have.

Because our brains are bombarded by thousands (maybe millions) of stimuli each day, when you come upon an idea, write it down. And since ideas seem to multiply in a sort of mental parthenogenesis, you'll probably end up with lots of lists.

To make sorting through them easier, give each list a name. One might be headed "Environment"; another, "Animal Rights." You may have a list called "City Government" and one called "Education."

Now, every other writer with op-ed ambitions will have lists headed "Environment," "Animal Rights," "City Government" and "Education" also. To cut through the competition, what you need to do is to come up with fresh angles, different approaches. Under "Education," for instance, instead of writing down ideas that have been op-eded to death—like lengthening the school day/year and paying premiums to good teachers—you might advocate compulsory preschool or multitracked education based on the students' aptitudes. Don't accept the first ideas that come into your mind. Write them down, to be sure. But refine them until they're nearer to original thought.

If your lists become too long, subdivide them into categories. File them in a folder labeled Op-Ed Ideas so that they're ready to turn to when you have your next thirty minutes of writing time.

THE RIGHT FIT

It's easiest to come up with workable ideas if you have particular op-ed markets in mind when you make your idea lists, since the subject matter must fit the intended publication.

As we've mentioned above, the more specialized a magazine's focus, the narrower the range of op-ed topics. About half of the publications listed in *Writer's Market* under the "Relationships" category, for example, say they use opinion pieces. Since those publications include *Bay Window* (for gays and lesbians), *Changing Men* (put out by Feminist Men's Publications) and *Foreskin Quarterly* (a magazine covering circumcision), it's pretty obvious that they're not looking for the same kinds of material.

Among the gay publications — and there are about half a dozen listed — subject matter runs across the spectrum of homosexual topics from *Guide to the Gay Northeast* to *DungeonMaster* (gay male erotic s/m).

When regional publications use op-eds, you can be sure they revolve around topics relevant to the regions they cover. The *Newsday* opinion section entry in *Writer's Market*, says, "Seeks opinion on current events, trends, issues — whether national or local government or life-style. Must be timely, pertinent, articulate and opinionated." *Southern Tier Images*, whose territory includes several counties in southern New York state, says, "All submissions must be strictly regional, pertaining to the Southern Tier of New York and surrounding areas only, or of particular interest to residents of these areas." Magazines listed under "Hobby and Crafts" and "Health and Fitness" have such diverse themes and readerships that their op-eds, too, must be specifically tailored to the publications.

It's not only important to determine the breadth of a publication's op-ed topics. In the case of newspapers, it's also vital to zero in on the scope. Do they extend beyond the community to the state, the nation, the world? Some papers prefer opinions about local leash laws to those on the proliferation of nuclear plants; others concern themselves only with national issues. Generally speaking, op-ed scope is a function of the paper's size and stature.

No idea—regardless of how fresh it is, whatever its breadth or scope—will be workable, however, unless you have a definite opinion about it. Most of us who are the least bit interested in writing op-eds, fortunately, have strong opinions on just about everything. We aren't fence-sitters.

Remember that discussion with your friend, Jack, about lowering capital gains taxes. At the outset, you thought you didn't give a darn since you're not particularly interested in economics. But once you started talking, the discussion turned into a debate as you thought of all sorts of reasons why people who profit from the sale of property ought to pay more instead of less.

If you're like me, that sort of thing happens a lot. Once we put our mind to a subject—really think about it—we realize that we do care; that we have an opinion supported by our observations and beliefs and, sometimes, by facts.

As far as facts are concerned, they're the stumbling block for many potential op-ed writers—especially the 30-Minute kind— most likely because fact-finding is the part of the project that's apt to take the most time.

In fact, the process shouldn't take you much time at all. Gathering the ammunition needed to support your op-ed contention can be done most efficiently with the aid of a good reference librarian at a public library. Just explain your project to the researcher, allow plenty of time ("I need it tomorrow" won't bring the results you want), and chances are, he or she will present you with a list of resources—or even have gathered them together.

All you will have to do is skim through the material and photocopy what you'll want to use—even the slightest chance it will be helpful is reason enough to copy it. Then, put all the pages in a file you can refer to whenever you get a hunk of free time. The only other research time you'll need is to check your facts and possibly to make a few phone calls.

Handling your research in thirty-minute increments is easier if, at the outset, you formulate a research game plan for the piece. During your first thirty-minute session, list the various pieces of information it appears that you will need (this list may be adjusted as you get into the project). After each item, write down possible sources for that information. Look up telephone numbers and addresses you'll need.

During each subsequent research session, choose one or two of the items on your list to investigate. Be realistic. Trying to accomplish an impossible amount of work in one session will frustrate you needlessly.

Any writer should do the utmost to insure accuracy of his or her facts and information, of course. But as an op-ed writer, there's further incentive. People who read the editorial page are generally far more critical than readership in general. They may be more intelligent as well. And quick to point out inaccuracies that leave writers with egg on their faces.

Which leads us to another quality potential op-ed writers must have: thick skin. If your work is picked out from all the rest and published, it's a triumph. But that triumph can turn to a minitragedy if you're shattered by the scathing letters to the editor that are certain to follow a controversial piece.

TAILORING TIPS

When your opinion pieces are rejected by the op-ed editors of your intended publications, it's impossible to tell whether the points of view were too off-the-wall or too wishy-washy, whether the points weren't developed or substantiated well enough, or whether the writing failed to meet the publication's standards.

It's very easy, though, to tell what sorts of op-eds those editors have considered worth buying. All you have to do is study the publications' back issues.

As far as style is concerned, it varies with the publication—from English-teacher formal in the more academic publications to breezy in publications that favor less serious subjects. As a writer, it's up to you to pick out a style that suits you and the publication best.

It's easy to determine the right word length. Establish a range by counting the words in three or four previously published op-eds in your intended magazine or newspaper; then aim for the place within the range that will best do justice to your opinion.

Pay heed, too, to adjectives, figures of speech and statistics. Chances are an op-ed with flowery descriptive passages and clichés won't gain acceptance anywhere. But any piece that's written in a style that's not in keeping with the publication's persona hasn't much hope either.

LEARNING EXPERIENCE

A good training ground for would-be op-ed writers is putting together letters to the editor. Start out with your local paper or regional magazine. Unless that publication prints every letter it receives, when you see the first of your submissions in print, try writing to a larger newspaper or magazine. When several of your letters have been printed—proof that your ideas are on target and your writing style is publishable—begin working on op-eds which in reality are only expanded versions of what you've been writing.

A growing number of newspapers have weekly awards for the best letter to the editor published during the period. Called everything from the "Golden Pen Award" to "Best Letter of the Week," they offer recognition but usually no cash.

Some newspapers have both a weekly op-ed page and an award for the best letter to the editor. The *Seattle Times* is one of them. In a recent Sunday paper, the op-ed on the paper's "Commentary and Opinion" page was titled "The View From the Sixth Grade" and ran with a banner reading "Why educational reform can't work." The piece was written by William Clow, a teacher at Chinook Middle School in Bellevue, Washington, and began like this:

> I am sitting in my classroom, finishing my lunch and listening to classical music on the radio as I wait for my first afternoon class to begin. It is a gloomy, rainy day and I can hear my sixth-graders mobbing the outside door and screaming at each other in shrill voices. In a few minutes they will storm in here and I will try to calm them down and seat them so we can begin a math lesson about adding and subtracting decimals.
>
> Of the 33 kids, I know that at least a dozen will not have done their homework. I know that half will fail the quiz and will not care. I also know that only a few will settle down finally, with my help, to begin their homework for tomorrow. For the next 45 minutes, some will scarcely stop their chatter with each other to focus on the work of the day.

In the next two paragraphs, Clow describes two parent-teacher conferences: one with a mother who berated the teacher for assigning work that was too hard for her son, the other with a father who demanded more challenging work for his daughter. He then goes on to address the "America 2000" program developed by President Bush and the state governors. His contention is that the program will fail, not because it is unrealistic, but because of parental and public opinion pressure.

Throughout the article, it is obvious that the writer is passionately interested and involved in his subject. He includes several examples — not only from his own experience but also from that of other teachers — of pressures placed on classroom teaching. The reader has no doubt about the writer's views or about why it was chosen as the op-ed piece of the week. The would-be writer who isn't yet ready to tackle a full-blown op-ed realizes that a similar topic would also be great for a letter to the editor.

Not only should you read op-eds in your quest for ideas, read them to learn how to write your own. But remember that op-ed pieces aren't all created equal. Some are created far more brilliantly than others, with just the right words setting forth the writer's thoughts and substantiating his viewpoint. Those are the ones to study.

One such op-ed, called "Trick or Trait?", appeared in the October 1991 issue of *Parenting*. Written by Laura Taxel, the piece is an excellent example of the tightly written, hard-hitting, and highly effective op-ed:

> Halloween has been getting scarier every year. It's not that ghosts are ghastlier or goblins more ghoulish—it's the girls. They all look like leftovers from a Miss America pageant: Gowns, crowns, and halos are de rigueur. From toddlers to teenagers, female trick-or-treaters in my neighborhood seem to be trapped in a time warp, their Halloween fantasies a throwback to an era I thought we'd left behind.
>
> Back in the fifties, long before Madonna made underwear outer wear, my most cherished costume fantasy revolved around a corset and a feather boa. I wanted to be a wild West dance hall girl. I didn't understand that a saloon girl was really a hooker; all I knew was that boys wanted to be cowboys and this was my idea of the female counterpart. That was, somehow, appropriate for the times.
>
> But since then, we've had the women's movement and men's groups. The age of Aquarius dawned, women hopped onto the fast track, and guys began doing dishes. So why do the kids coming to my door look just like we did 35 years ago?
>
> I'm not exaggerating. A steady stream of princesses, brides, fairies, and angels ring the bell and earnestly ask for goodies. Sometimes there are girl witches, but they are always cute. The boys, on the other hand, usually bypass cute in favor of a weapon-toting swagger just as they did when I was a kid. They are pirates, spacemen, and monsters. They choose to be superheroes and universe-masters. When boys masquerade they portray males who Do, who Can. They become little men of action, or powerful, terrifying monsters.
>
> Today's little girls may be free to wear overalls and play with trucks, but when it comes to expressing their fantasies, they still

come out pink and pretty. In their glitter and flounces, they join the time-honored female tradition of do-nothing loveliness: Saloon girl or sprite, they haven't much power. Indeed, every time I ask a little girl if she's a queen, she assures me she is a princess. And why not? Queens, I have deduced, possess a certain unwelcome authority, and of course, they may not be pretty. They might be evil or, heaven help us, old.

Last year, a ten-year-old girl I know chose to be a French maid, complete with a dress that barely covered and a black velvet bow at her throat that looked more like a dog collar than a decoration. Her mother wondered where she'd gone wrong: Her daughter had opted not only for beauty but for subjugation, too.

While my generation supposedly repudiated the standard role-model stereotypes, this girl's fantasy and my old one have much in common, and I can't help but wonder what is at work here: X and Y chromosomes, youthful rebellion, reactionary parents, the break-down of the American family, or archetypal truths? How can to-day's young girls remain so untouched by all the years of women trying to change their image?

But as I ruminated last Halloween, I was reminded of my own childhood by a pre-schooler, sex unknown, who came to the door dressed as a pumpkin. My mother used to do that to me. Not having any idea of what I really wanted to be, she made me clever costumes that I hated. One year she dressed me in paper bags, and made a bird's nest, complete with bird, for me to wear in my hair. I was a tree. I won a prize. I was miserable; I wanted beauty and glamour.

I still do, I realize. If I were to receive an invitation to a masquer-ade party today, I would not dream of going as a tree or an ugly old hag. Who among us, liberated though we may be, can say that she has abandoned all her dreams of youth and beauty?

More important, it occurs to me that trick-or-treaters may *look* the same as they did in my youth, but feel differently about them-selves and who they will be in life. After all, a costume is about appearances. And if we have learned anything during these past 20-plus years of female consciousness-raising, it is that men and women must be treated as whole beings, and that a woman is much more than her looks. The girls on my front porch may want to look gorgeous, but nonetheless intend to become mountain climbers and scientists; the boys may masquerade as powerful demons, but even so expect to be warm and gentle fathers. For just as women are greater than the sum of their body measurements, I know the trick-or-treaters I see are more than the dreams they dress up in one night a year.

Maybe you won't write such a well-crafted op-ed the first or second or sixth time around. Most people don't. But keep at it and your skills as an op-ed writer will reflect the effort.

Be sure your premise is stated clearly in the article's lead. Sufficiently document each point you make so that it's convincing. Ruthlessly slash any extraneous material. Be scrupulous about sentence structure and take pains to see that your material flows from one point to the next in a logical sequence. Spend time constructing a good ending, one worthy of your opinion.

If you doubt your qualifications, just read the op-ed authors' minibios. You'll find that a good percentage of them are written by freelancers and people who were formerly editors and columnists of various publications. Others are attorneys or doctors; bartenders or auto mechanics — people who are facile with words and have something worth saying. People like you.

THE 30-MINUTE WRITER'S PLAN OF ACTION

1. Spend your first session in self-analysis, deciding if you have the motivation/commitment to write op-ed pieces and, if so, what subjects you care strongly enough about to justify the time you'll spend.

2. Cut out or photocopy op-eds from a variety of publications. Choose several that you think would be likely markets for your subjects. Then, as best as you can, weigh the chances of success for each of these topics. Are the ideas fresh, timely, well thought out? Would the subjects be of interest to

a broad spectrum of the publications' readers? Can you come up with enough supporting material to justify your position? Go with the one that seems most likely to be a winner.

3. Develop a research plan, as suggested earlier in the chapter, to gather needed information.

4. Begin structuring your op-ed, using previously published opinion pieces in your targeted publication as a pattern; for example, Opening lead (2 paragraphs), First substantiating point and supporting evidence (2 paragraphs), Second substantiating point and supporting evidence (3 paragraphs), Third substantiating point and summarizing evidence (3 paragraphs), Closing, using quote if possible (1 or 2 paragraphs).

5. When you have finished writing, set the piece aside for a time.

6. Spend your final thirty-minute session going over the article one more time. You'll be amazed at the ease with which you will be able to strengthen it after having let the piece rest for a few days.

CHAPTER VI

Laughing
Matter

It's not funny. The pace of life in our part of the world seems to accelerate by the decade. It takes a lot of energy just to carve out enough hours in the day. Meanwhile, we worry a lot — about recession, inflation, pollution, responsibilities of job and family. Life can be grim.

But as I remember it, the essayists of yore were always advising us to turn adversity into advantage. And who should be better able to turn the adversity of pressure-cooker life into an outlet for his or her writing wares than the 30-Minute Writer with a sense of fun. For difficult times and humor do go together. If we can have a good laugh, we won't want so much to cry.

In fact, the more dismal the situation, the greater the editorial clamor for humorous articles and columns. Through the years, as we've collectively worried about the cold war, various famines, Mideast instability and the national debt, writers like syndicated columnists Dave Barry and Art Hoppe and humorists Roy Blount, Jr., and Erma Bombeck have given us balance by making us grin.

By turning on your laugh-making machine and learning how to string your printed words together so that they make people chuckle, you can come up with a product that's irresistible to both editors and readers.

When the harried computer programmer/commuter, frazzled airport controller/parent, and hassled convenience store clerk finally make it home and decide to read a magazine rather than doze in front of the TV, chances are their choices of reading material won't be heavy. If they can have a few laughs along the way, you — the writer — will have lightened up their day. Editors know this.

As 30-Minute Writers, you'll find humorous articles appealing for a variety of reasons. To start with, researching the markets by finding publications that use humorous articles and then reading those articles is fun — it lets you feel like you're getting something accomplished without pain. Then, too, the articles themselves don't require serious research. They may involve some casual interviews with entertaining people, but that's all. Most of your effort will consist of the kind of "think" time that's like a game. If your idea's really funny, you'll get a lot of laughs while you're thinking.

But just because you decide to write humor doesn't mean you should take the job lightly. First of all, you need to know the differences among the various forms your frivolous prose might take:

1. *Light humor.* That gentle fun-poking at our human natures is the best-seller. It's the form of humor you'll find in most general interest magazines and specialized publications that appeal to mainstream America.

2. *Irony.* As a humor form, irony seems to be gaining in popularity. It involves saying exactly what you don't mean. I, personally, find the form mildly entertaining if used in small doses. However, irony can so easily drift into sarcasm and become tedious. Its effectiveness is greatest if you use it to close your piece; for example, an article jabbing at inflexible hospital routines might end with "Aren't appendectomies fun?"

3. *Exaggeration.* Take any facet of everyday life — usually a frustrating one — and exaggerate the way people react to it. Waiting for repairmen, having to write using nongender language, locking your keys in the car, calls at the dinner hour from people who want to clean your carpet — your choice of potential subjects is limited only by your imagination.

4. *Satire*. Probably the hardest form of humor to pull off—at least, to write well. Satire's subjects are usually things that aren't funny at all: the high cost of funerals, financial fraud, society's excesses, and so on. Most of the best contemporary satire you will read appears in magazines with well-educated readers.

5. *Parody*. Take any well-known story, movie plot or event and imitate it in style and content, using a different subject. For instance, you might write a piece in the style of the antebellum genre about embarrassing moments when men have lost their toupees called "Gone With the Wind."

6. *Off-the-Wall*. Look at a subject upside-down, sideways, from a totally crazy angle. Examine the ordinary in an extraordinary light. Be as zany as you like. Whether you can sell an off-the-wall piece or not, you'll have a lot of fun thinking about it.

For instance, I was once involved in a volunteer project putting together a church brochure—complete with pictures—that explained the congregation's activities. The committee got so involved in zany ideas that we produced both the requisite brochure and an underground edition, a totally irreverent, off-the-wall spoof that could never have been published, let alone circulated. However, even nonpublishable works have value. They get your mind going in a humorous direction, so that you can see something that's laughable in just about every situation.

I JUST GOT THIS FUNNY IDEA

One humorist I know maintains that the ideas for funny articles are everywhere. You just have to know how to look at them. Many of the subjects used by the most widely read humorists are mundane, in fact. I recall a piece by Erma Bombeck about trying on clothes, several others about carpooling and going to the grocery store. Back-to-school night, a business lunch where everything went wrong, trying to change the zoning on a piece of property—none of them sound like ha-ha stuff, but . . .

1. The cardinal rule of idea gathering is not to let any ideas

get away. Good, bad or indifferent, write those ideas down on paper when they occur and before they float away to the land of nondocumented thoughts. Also write down brief descriptions of funny things you see: strange signs, really good bumper stickers and license plates, odd listings on menus.

The next trick is to put your idea sheets in a place where you can find them easily or, better yet, a place where you'll run across them even when you're not looking. After you have accumulated a number of these idea sheets, you'll often find that several of the items fit into the same category (or could be rearranged slightly so that they do): funny things that have happened in the kitchen, at the fitness center, in parking lots; funny sights you have seen at the shopping mall or a certain square downtown.

After you have collected a fair number of compatible items, start thinking of the ways you can write about them. Take shopping malls, for example. Just offhand, I can think of several ideas for humorous articles based on notes jotted down at odd moments in all parts of the world (including one in Turku, Finland, where my hotel room balcony looked out on the interior of a large, indoor shopping mall with essence of french fries wafting through the balcony door).

For starters, I might do a piece on "mall rats," the kids who hang out at malls everywhere, including that mall in Finland. Or maybe one on mall entertainments, which can be pretty funny if you have a bizarre enough sense of humor. Mall fights (second only to those that go on in parking lots), mall food and mall sales are spoofable, too. And again back to that mall hotel in Finland—how about an article on strange hotel locations.

Whenever something funny happens, make notes about it as soon as you can. Some incidents—like the time a Kowloon restroom lock jammed and no one who could help me spoke English—stay in your memory forever. But other snippets of life that could be used effectively in humorous articles aren't quite so memorable.

Be equally attentive to funny stories people tell you about things that have happened to them. You might want to incorporate them into article ideas or use them as anecdotal material. Be sure to write down the source of each of these stories. If you don't, you'll be frustrated when you want more information in the future.

2. If possible, team up with a writer friend who likes to laugh. One of mine, Marge Knorr, writes great humor. Whenever the two of us go anyplace—to the big ethnic food market in Reno, to art exhibits and community celebrations—it's a sure thing that we will find lots of things to laugh at. And laughing together gives both of us ideas of things to write about.

Not all of our hilarious adventures lead to article sales, however. A case in point was the "First Annual" Great American Kiss-Off held in Reno a few autumns ago. To our minds, one of the funniest events ever held (a few of our friends described it as disgusting), it was a competition to see which of a dozen or so couples could stay joined at the lips longest. It took place each day from 9 A.M. to 9 P.M. in a damaged freight store's parking lot (kind of funny in itself). About three weeks into the competition, two of the couples decided to tie the knot at a public wedding. The night before the ceremony, a third couple—she was eight and a half months pregnant—decided to get married, too.

We took rolls of film, pages of interviews with couples during the short breaks they were allowed, searched vainly for an interested publication and were still hunting when the affair ended amidst much controversy and hard feelings. Needless to say, it did not become an annual event.

3. Spend some "think time" with pen and pad close by. Choose uninterrupted half hours away from distractions. Let your mind ramble through everyday life, concentrating on frustrations one session, ridiculous customs and trends, the next. And be sure to set aside a session or two devoted

to food, for eating is one of the most popular topics for humorous pieces.

During the frustration session, think primarily about things that bug not only you, but lots of other people as well, such as patronizing waiters, parents whose children are perfect, people who insist on appropriating both armrests of the middle seats on airplanes.

On ridiculous trends day, remember that it isn't a good idea to denigrate any group, but it certainly is fair game to poke fun at society in general. Remember, too, that specific customs people in your age, societal or demographic group consider bizarre are totally accepted by people in others, so you'll want to focus on the concept rather than the custom or fad itself.

4. Watch TV. It's funny—not always when it is supposed to be and usually when it isn't. So don't stay tuned to a boring sitcom unless you want to write a funny piece on nonfunny TV. Watch programs that make you laugh and analyze why. Ask yourself if any of the ideas could be recycled into articles. Pay attention to the ads. Which of them could be used to illustrate a piece on TV advertising? When they're clever, what was done to make them so?

5. Read the papers, especially those in small towns; they can give you a lifetime's worth of humor article ideas. One I have in mind—but will probably never write—focuses on dangling participles and other misplaced parts of speech.

The first glimmer of the idea for it came from an article I read in the Detroit Lakes, Minnesota, paper. The piece told of a woman who was abducted by her ex-husband. It closed with the sentence, "[man's name] drove [woman's name] to [location] in northern Becker County where she was tied to a tree by her neck and left behind."

THE QUESTION OF TASTE

Even in this day of liberated language, what's considered suitable for the readers for one publication will make the editors of less linguistically emancipated publications shudder.

This purity of prose doesn't apply only to religious publications. Several of the lower circulation women's magazines—the kind that have pen pal pages—appeal to conservative, unsophisticated audiences.

Then, too, keep in mind that some nine and ten year olds read magazines like *Sports Illustrated* and *Good Housekeeping* cover to cover. The editors of any magazines—especially those perceived as "family"—aren't going to jeopardize their circulation figures by including any material that a sizable segment of the readership might consider objectionable.

WHO CAN DO IT

Some experts maintain that writing humorous material isn't a craft that can be taught; that it is a talent some people have and others don't—like it's genetic and you're born being funny and grow up able to write that way. I disagree.

Obviously, some people view life so seriously that their entire personalities would have to change for them to even want to write humor. But people who can write and have a sense of humor should be able to produce funny stuff. Maybe not laugh-until-your-stomach-aches material, but at least words that will make readers smile inside.

Writing humor, whether it be subtle or not, does require that you pay attention to the rules. The following will give you a good idea of what they are:

1. Don't tell readers that something is funny. Use words to show them that it is. You start out with a title such as Marge Knorr's "Food for Thought: Are Mormon crickets pests or protein? We bug the experts," which appeared in *Nevada* Magazine. Then, like Knorr did, amplify the title with a lead that's a grabber:

    Nutritionists are no fun. They're so busy telling us what to eat that they've missed something right under their noses— bugs.

The paragraphs that follow continue in the same vein. None of them say "I'm funny" but instead, show that they are.

"I know zip about eating insects," confessed one University of Nevada, Reno nutritionist I talked to. "Not me," said another assistant professor of nutrition. "I'd never eat insects. I'm too deeply immersed in my own culture."

On the other hand, Gary Blomquist, an insect biochemist at UNR, didn't hesitate to give his opinion: "Termites, they're the best, deep-fat fried with bitter almond sauce on the side."

Years ago, while visiting a famous city that shall remain nameless, I had lunch at an expensive, fashionable restaurant. I was dazzled by the glitter and sophistication.

When my salad arrived, I picked up the chilled fork, ready to savor the prelude to the meal. Then something moved in the greenery. A critter jumped from my plate onto the white-linen tablecloth. Shrieking, I leaped to my feet, sophistication and chic forgotten. It was a grasshopper. Yuk!

Recalling this recently, I began wondering about our aversion to insects as food. Was it advisable to eat invertebrates?

After all, last year was a banner year for creepy-crawlies. The Mormon cricket infestation around Winnemucca made national headlines, exasperated farmers and ranchers, and gave birth to a new industry, Mormon cricket T-shirts. Meanwhile, there were yellow jackets in South Lake Tahoe, aphids in Los Angeles, killer bees in Texas, Mediterranean fruit flies in California and Florida, and cicadas in Illinois.

I decided to bug the experts.

With the stage thus set, Knorr gets into the serious, yet funny, business of her piece, telling about insects as food — historically, nutritionally, in other cultures and in our own. She not only informs readers, she entertains them every word of the way.

2. Don't use unnecessary words. We all know people who love to tell jokes, but cannot resist digressing every now and then, so that even if it was not meant to be a shaggy dog, the story ends up that way. Keep your writing clean.

For example, were I writing about my Kowloon restroom experience, I might say:

It was a muggy day in Kowloon so my friend and I had decided to take a cab to the Sheraton Hotel for dim sum lunch. When we got there we asked where the restaurant was and were told it was on the top floor (my guidebook said it was on the main floor near the lobby). When we arrived at the restaurant we found out that lunch wouldn't be served for another ten minutes, so I went to the restroom. When I tried to leave, I found that the lock was jammed. What was I going to do?

I might say that, but it wouldn't sell. Instead, I would say:

High atop what I thought was the Kowloon Sheraton in a restroom with a jammed lock, I considered my options.

3. Write visually. When we're involved in face-to-face conversation and tell a funny story, our voice inflections, pacing, gestures, facial expression and timing of the punch line all add to the performance. When writing that same story, we have fewer devices. That means we must write so the reader "sees" the action.

4. Give your piece an appropriate title that's clever. While editors are usually adept at changing titles on nonhumorous articles, they don't generally do as well with the funny ones. By providing a good title to start with, you'll insure that your piece is a laugh from beginning to end.

One title I especially like was in *Image*, the Sunday newspaper magazine. The piece was called "Voulez Vous Voucher Avec Moi?" with the subtitle "Even in a limo, you're nobody without a pink slip."

5. Concentrate on placing your words. Sequence can influence emphasis as much as the words themselves. For example, "Nice work if you can get it" has a snappier ring than "If you can get that kind of work, it's nice." Early in my career, a writer whose work I greatly respected, told me never to use an exclamation point. "If you have to resort to an Oh-My-Gosh mark," he said, "you aren't putting your words in the right order."

6. Know when to stop. As mentioned before, satire and sarcasm can become tedious. So can any other kind of humor when it is overwritten. Get to your punchline and then exit.

7. Leave 'em laughing. This may seem contradictory, coming after the last paragraph. But all punchlines aren't funny. Sometimes they need a zippy sentence or two to round the article off.

Humor often has its sad side—remember Red Skelton in his clown routine. When you write a humorous piece that involves pathos, triste or even angst, end it on the upbeat. Otherwise, it won't be humor.

The simple sentence ending ("Did I get even with him," "Maybe birthdays are supposed to be that way," or "I'll try again tomorrow") is the most popular humor ending you're apt to find when you study previously published articles. More often than not, that last sentence ties in with something that was said in the first paragraphs of the piece. Remember when Marge Knorr talked about the grasshopper in her salad? Here's how she ended the piece:

For myself, I've decided that if I ever again have a grasshopper in my salad at a fancy restaurant, I'll try to keep my cool. I'll nonchalantly ask the waitperson to take it back to the kitchen and "please toast it lightly, but hold the mayo." Still, there remains another question. Which is the correct fork for eating insects?

TO MARKET

In writing humor, as with other kinds of articles, it's best to identify your market first and then decide what kind of a piece you're going to write. Your chances increase dramatically when you submit a funny, well-written article that fits the magazine's content. The subject and style, readership's background and educational level all have to be considered.

Although there are few editors who don't welcome articles written with a light touch, the gradations of humor range from the really subtle to the kind you read in *Mad* magazine. Therefore, some self-analysis is necessary in looking for markets for your humorous material. Just how funny are you?

The best approach is to find out which magazines' articles make you laugh. We all don't identify with the same kinds of humor and it's tough to write any kind of article that doesn't seem in sync with your psyche.

After you've identified publications whose humor you enjoy, start thinking about subjects parallel to those their editors have favored in the past. The published humor in any magazine can be analyzed this way, as long as you have four to six back copies. The more recent copies you have, the more certain you can be that your analysis is on the mark. You'll also have a better idea of the limits on subject matter.

Choosing parallel ideas is probably the easiest way to come up with the subject to write about for your targeted publication. And you will, in most cases, have to write the whole article. Query letters, which are acceptable or required at most magazines for nonfiction articles, don't work for humor.

You can't write a letter to the editor saying "I would like to write a very funny article about inchworms" and expect to be taken at your word. Funny to you may mean something very different from funny to the editor. You have to show him that your sense of humor coincides with his.

You don't have to produce material that will make them roll in the aisles, but if you can give readers reason to smile a little, most editors will find it difficult to turn your well-written material down.

For this chapter's last laugh, here's a piece by Jim Andersen that appeared in *Nevada*, whose editor and art director have a great sense of humor. The article was illustrated with a zany photo of four people around a campfire, their roasted marshmallows aflame.

While you're reading, notice how easily the article flows. You aren't required to do anything but read—no big words you don't quite understand to get in the way, lots of variation in sentence length, and punctuation that makes the longer sentences easy to follow. Humor is dispensed throughout the piece, not just a shot here or there. Some of the statements are made outrageous by the almost/never approach; for example, "Mountain roads don't go anywhere."

The experiences Andersen writes about in "Rules You Can Camp On" are universal. Even if a person has never been camping, he or she can still relate to dirt, bug bites and sunburn. Every reference, every description is so visual that you can picture what's being written about. And Anderson has massaged his words so that each one falls into the place where it will add the most to the humorous whole.

Some people can spend hours talking about camping and trading tips about ground cloths and tent pegs. But I don't believe there is any such thing as a really great camping trip.

If you are a traditional American camper who uses sleeping bags and flashlights and folding spoons, at some point you're going to wind up wet and cold and miserable, with wood smoke stinging your eyes and no-see-ums nesting in your scalp, and there's nothing you or God or President Bush can do about it.

Fortunately, though, enjoyment doesn't require comfort. If it did, people wouldn't voluntarily get on roller coasters. And they sure wouldn't go camping.

Keeping that in mind, you can tip the odds a little if you understand the rules that come into play the moment you leave your driveway:

1. There are no good campsites. The best campsites of a couple of hundred years ago are cities today. What's left over is, well, left over, so it's usually dumb to pass by the first likely campsite you see. If it's level enough that your bedroll doesn't go bouncing down into the creek, and if there's a tree around somewhere, it's about as good as you can expect.

2. Mountain roads don't go anywhere. Well, OK, some do, but most—probably around 89 percent—either are severed by 20-foot washouts or blunder into the middle of mosquito-infested swamps.

In order to turn around, you need to find a place at least as wide as your vehicle is long, the nearest being about a mile back down the road. There's nothing to be done about this because there apparently is another rule that makes it mandatory for campers to drive up every interesting road they come upon.

3. Roughing it builds character. It really does. People who routinely rise up to counter adversity with initiative even without access to a True Value hardware store, got that way by tackling problems in the wilderness with their chins held high. They're always cheerful, industrious, uncomplaining, and, for the most part, they make me sick.

However, if you want to be that sort of person, I'd suggest you get one of those pressurized pump-up camp stoves. You'll build character on the scope of Mahatma Gandhi.

4. The bugs own the outdoors. When camping, it's not how you keep away from the bugs, but how you keep them away from you.

I have tried, singly and in unison, liquid repellents, spray foggers, and great billowy clouds of smoke manufactured by burning green wood, highway flares, and old tires. The bugs initially run for cover, but they're usually back before I regain consciousness. In the end, all you can do is treat the bites.

5. There is no way to avoid sunburn. You can stay in the shade all day. You can apply sunscreen with a pan and roller. You can

wear a tarpaulin. No matter, you're going to get burned red like a lobster.

I have never seen a camper who wasn't sunburned, and I suspect the sun's rays are sucked into a camp the way leaves are sucked into a whirlpool. I guess if you want to stay out of the sun, stay out of the camp.

6. Dirt is your friend. So is soot from the fire, and ashes. Ashes have a particular affinity for fried potatoes, or maybe they just show up better, so I leave 'em in there.

They are not very tasty, and I take that as an indication that ashes are probably very good for you. Dirt, which is more versatile, can be worn, eaten, and slept with. And will be.

7. Mishaps will converge on one person per camp. It's not always the same person, either. It seems to be a random selection based solely on the luck of the draw, and I hate it when it's me. Once, on a weekend trip up Mount Whitney, I ended up with a bee sting, blistered feet, swollen knees, forehead contusions from a run-in with a tent pole, and a goose egg from a chunk of falling ice. Nothing at all happened to my three companions.

If you happen to know a person who consistently attracts this sort of thing, you should definitely invite him or her along.

8. Camping is not an activity. When it's not irritating, camping is incredibly boring. All there is to do between meals is sit around in a lawn chair and watch the creek gurgle past while you swat flies. Fishing is an activity, and so is hiking and even reading, but you can't pin your vacation plans solely on camping, because camping is the original uncola.

9. Camping takes place in a different time zone. Darkness falls faster, and lasts longer, in camp than it does in civilization. That's because darkness evokes a primal fear within us, which in turn slows time in direct proportion to the amount of bejeesus that is being scared out of us at any particular moment. Which, in the inky wilderness, can be quite a bit.

10. It is acceptable to chicken out. The only thing more pathetic than packing it in and running for a motel is pretending you know how to cope with mud slides and other natural disasters. Mother

Nature can be very enjoyable, but she's not always kind, and that's why man has spent the last several thousand years trying to insulate himself from her vagaries.

The completed product is called, I believe, a Winnebago.

Not only is the preceeding article well crafted, it is proof that you don't need to live in Bigtime America, just blocks from the nearest comedy club, to write great humor. Jim Andersen's home is in Austin, Nevada (pop. 300), a town that's miles from anywhere, on a highway known as "The Loneliest Road in America."

THE 30-MINUTE WRITER'S PLAN OF ACTION

1. Whenever you read a humorous article that makes you laugh, clip it out (or photocopy it) along with the magazine's cover and masthead, which lists the editors' names and the publication's address. If the piece is in a newspaper, attach the name of the newspaper and its date in lieu of a cover. This process will serve two purposes, providing both good examples to study and market information.

2. Make lists of common items and events — after-shave lotions, trendy clothes, birthday parties, high school dances — that have their funny side. Certain places lend themselves to humor, too. Choose two or three that you like best and start rolling them around in your brain. Also, pair them up with possible markets. If the editor of Magazine A has run funny articles about shopping at garage sales and cleaning out the refrigerator, she'll probably go for one about do-it-yourself plumbing or trying to grow tropical plants in your bathroom.

3. Carry a small notebook with you at all times, not only to jot down inspirations for the pieces you've decided to write, but also to note funny things that happen in the course of each day and might become the basis for or part of future articles.

4. Put the main points of your article on paper. Don't censor

yourself. Just write. The easiest way to stifle humor is by becoming self-critical. There will be rough spots, sure. But you can smooth them out later.

5. Work on your article a section at a time. Examine each sentence to see if you've maximized its humor. Keep pacing in mind. Remember that what comedians say isn't as funny as the way they say it.

6. After you've worked on a piece for a while, it may stop sounding funny. Put it away for a week or so. If it's good, you'll start laughing again.

CHAPTER VII

Hot Tips

While we 30-Minute Writers have, to varying degrees, become shortcut specialists (and dollar shavers, too), many of us haven't yet learned to become successful tipsters. We haven't tried capitalizing on our timesaving strategies by writing them up and sending them off to magazines that buy hints and tips.

These guides to everyday efficiency and problem solving are the easiest short-short items to write and the least time-consuming. They're usually only a sentence or two in length—just long enough to give the reader a hint on how to save money when having the poodle clipped or save time when cleaning the car.

Ideas for these tips are right in our kitchens, offices, workshops and gardens. They sometimes require a bit of experimentation, but as far as research is concerned, that's all.

Granted, pay for solutions to the little problems of everyday life won't solve the big problems of paying for the kids' orthodontia or the month's groceries. But the five-, twenty- and even hundred-dollar checks that come regularly to writers who have mastered the trick of tip writing will buy a lot of extra treats.

TOPICAL TIPS

When you discover a new way of doing something, don't dismiss it by thinking, "That's so elementary, anyone could figure it out." I say this from sad experience. I've had many ideas I thought were too ordinary to submit, only to see them in print six months later with someone else's byline.

But how can you be sure that your tips don't duplicate those that have already been printed? You can never tell for sure. You will, however, know that your idea has a chance if 1.) you originated it or 2.) you got it from another source but have refined the idea or combined it with another.

To generate all sorts of tip ideas, the next time you have an extra thirty minutes, use it to walk through your home, shop or office. Spend some time in each room, thinking about what you do there, how you have saved time on some jobs and what you might do to streamline others.

Look around my kitchen with me, and you'll see how the process works:

On my kitchen desk is a pile of checkout receipts from the supermarket and other stores. When I have collected fifteen or twenty of them, I turn them to their blank sides, staple them at the top and have a handy, no-cost tablet on which to write grocery lists. That tip has a good chance of selling.

In my freezer are cubes of frozen lemon juice, each just the right size for making a glass of lemonade. Though they're convenient, the idea doesn't seem innovative enough for a tip.

As you become aware of hints that are printed in various publications, you'll realize that some tips—such as "Remove ballpoint pen marks with shampoo"—have been used by every household hints authority from Heloise to Mary Ellen. But it's sometimes difficult to determine whether your own ideas are original enough. A good way to test your tips is by checking them out with friends. Chances are, if they've heard or read similar ones, they'll tell you.

Although the lemonade cubes idea is pretty common, what about the homemade soup that's also in the freezer?

I freeze meal-sized portions in a kettle and then store the frozen soup rounds in plastic bags. When I want to serve the soup, I simply slip the frozen rounds into the same kettle and heat. That tip could sell . . . and it did.

I keep kitchen wipes in a drawer but rarely use them in the

kitchen. Instead, I take them traveling. They become lap cloths for hotel-room snacks, washcloths in countries where those niceties aren't provided, or turban-style shower caps. The basic idea here is a good one, but the concept needs a couple more suggestions for using the towels before it will be ready to submit.

Our breakfast place mats are recycled, an old set made new by pasting postcard collages on top of the mats and then coating them in plastic. That idea might sell, especially if you suggest pictures of grandchildren for grandparents' place mats or of storybook characters for kiddies.

I line wicker plant holders with the bottom portions of plastic water jugs, use plastic berry boxes as frogs for large flower arrangements. Big cookie cutters are great for making fun-shaped pancakes after they're fried (grown-ups eat the scraps). A spice bottle that I've filled with the proper proportions of cinnamon, ginger and cloves helps pumpkin pie making go faster.

In my pantry and fridge are jars of dry pancake, biscuit and hot drink mixes made from scratch with instructions as to what ingredients to add taped to each jar. With a little bit of experimentation, I know I could figure out more unusual (and therefore, more salable) mixes that would save readers — and me — time and money.

Within the kitchen cupboards, clutter is on the ragged edge of becoming chaos. But a few thirty-minute "think" sessions would come up with dollars' worth of ideas for making storage space more efficient. This brainstorming time might also generate ideas for innovative ways to reuse plastic and paper items — and recycling tips are among today's best-sellers.

Like my home and office, your environment has been made more efficient by innovative ideas that you've generated. You, too, have space or time or money problems. Their solutions, when put into the appropriate formats, in many cases will be salable.

But hints and tips don't always involve physical objects. They concern people and relationships, too. Getting kids to eat their vegetables, stop fighting and do their chores; ways to raise money for the school library, to stay in touch with friends who have moved away, to give gifts that have special meaning — if your ideas are fresh, these tip-topics are sure to be editorial hits.

Another idea generator involves making lists. Use such headings as Children, Garden, Cost-Cutting, Cleaning, Entertaining, Sewing and Car. Under each heading jot down any jobs you have made easier, ways you have saved money, problems you've coped with successfully. Include problems you haven't solved and experiment with solutions.

You'll find the time spent is doubly worthwhile. Not only will you have made your own life easier, but you'll also be paid for your efforts when you sell your tips.

Your list headed Entertaining might look something like this. Fill in your own solutions and use them as the bases for your tips that others can use as well.

Entertaining

Problem	Solution
Getting guests to come to the table	
Staying within a tight budget	
Finding time to cook	
House/apartment is too small	
Husband's friends don't like mine	

The list headed Car might read:

Problem	Solution
Buying one — getting best value	
Teenagers — fair sharing	
Remembering to put gas cap back on	
Repair costs	
Kids' clutter	
Remembering to have it serviced	
Anything to do with safety	

Another list might be headed Disposables. Skyhook a little and write down all the uses you can think for each item, no matter how far out.

Take plastic margarine tubs, for instance, or plastic gift ribbon spools or cardboard paper towel cylinders. What about the egg-shaped panty hose containers? If you can think up original, practical uses for any of them, you're on your way to a sale. Spawning ideas will become a sort of game that you'll play automatically as you get into the swing of writing hints and tips.

The best tips I've come up with have been a result of conversations with friends. Once, at a dinner party, the hostess brought out a scrapbook of her latest trip. Each page of the scrapbook was dated and held mementos of the day's events under its plastic sheets. I combined that idea with another (putting each day's souvenirs into a different manila envelope while traveling) and sold the item to *Family Circle* for twenty-five dollars (they now pay one hundred dollars for similar material).

HINTS ON SELLING TIPS

Once you've become hooked on hinting, you'll be on the alert not only for ideas to sell but also for places to send them. To find out which publications use hints and tips, first go skim the listings in *Writer's Market* (they will appear after the Fillers heading under the names of the individual publications).

Indicate potential markets in the book's margins. I mark each one "H&T" with an asterisk following those that seem especially promising. Then, when a bit of time comes along, I send for sample copies of the magazines that seem to fit in with the scope of my abilities and interests. I wouldn't, for example, send for a copy of the *Home Shop Machinist*, which specifies a need for "machining tips/shortcuts," since I barely understand how machine tools work.

Many of the publications listed in *Writer's Market* that use hints and tips don't, however, specify that they do. So continue your market research by leafing through every magazine you can get your hands on. In some magazines, the tips appear in a regular department and fill entire pages. In others, they're scattered throughout the publication.

Just because you don't see the particular department for an issue or two, don't assume that it has been discontinued. For instance, at *Better Homes and Gardens*, the "Family Network" department is considered part of the Health & Education portion of the magazine. During months like November and December, when the magazine is full of holiday features, Health & Education copy shrinks to make room for the seasonal material. That means there often isn't space for the hints and tips in those particular issues.

The hints and tips that are scattered throughout a magazine are harder to spot when you're doing your market research. Chances are, though, that the competition will be less intense because not so many other writers will have taken the time to discover them.

You'll also see hints and tips in newspapers. Assume that they are produced by staffers unless they're grouped together and/or you see a solicitation of items from readers.

A market most freelancers don't even think about is that composed of product manufacturers. If, for example, you have found an unusual use for cleanser or for plastic bags, write the manufacturers to ask if they pay for tips on uses for their products. If their replies are affirmative, send them your submissions.

Editors of magazines that use hints and tips (and of some magazines that don't) receive dozens of submissions each month and can use only a small fraction of them. High-visibility publications such as *Woman's Day* and *Family Circle* get hundreds. According to "Neighbors" department editor Lynne Zerance, the figure is about four hundred a month at *Woman's Day*. Katrina Mucha, who is in charge of the "Between Friends" pages at *Family Circle*, also reports that her department receives hundreds of submissions.

Though the odds are horrendous, don't let them keep you from submitting. Zerance says that the reason ideas make the cut at her magazine is that "they're original; something I haven't read in fifty other letters. And they are ideas that could help many of our readers. We receive some great ideas that we have to reject because they're so specific they wouldn't apply to a broad readership."

Amy Elbert, managing editor of *Friendly Exchange* (published quarterly), says she receives "two hundred to three hundred submissions and uses from six to ten per issue." Like Zerance, Elbert says that the major reason tips hit the rejection pile is that they're not original. Also, she says, some of the tips are too technical or too involved.

REFINING YOUR RAW TIP MATERIAL

You will increase your handy helps' chances of being among the "select" group by putting them into the form your intended publication uses. That way, the editor won't have to do anything to your copy but pass it along to the printer. And editors delight in working with writers who send them hassle-free material.

In analyzing hints and tips, you'll notice that those in paragraph form usually begin in one of six ways:

1. With an imperative verb: "Fill a net vegetable bag," "Sew soap scraps," "Spray furniture polish . . ."
2. With an adverbial phrase: "When driving in the rain," "While washing the dinner dishes . . ."
3. With an infinitive phrase: "To keep sheets smelling fresh," "To teach children good manners," "To weatherproof your dogs . . ."
4. With a statement defining the problem or setting forth the tip, followed by explanatory sentences that develop the idea in detail: "Setting deadlines for teenagers can start no-win arguments"; "Eating alone in a restaurant makes many women feel self-conscious."
5. With a conditional clause: "If you want to avoid post-Christmas bills," "Whether you live in a city apartment or country farmhouse . . ."
6. With a summarizing sentence: "I like saving recipes clipped from magazines and have solved the problem of keeping them in order"; "We enjoy eating out as a family, but rising prices have made the cost prohibitive."

Though some hints and tips departments use material written with all six types of beginnings, a number of publications such as *Woman's World* lean heavily toward the imperative verb lead: "Toss a couple of denture tablets in the toilet . . ."; "Have everyone in the family brush their teeth in the shower . . ."; "Use liquid soap dispensers . . ."; "Have a three-tier wire mesh basket. . . ."

A few publications present their tips in the problem/solution structure. This format sets out **The Problem** or THE QUESTION in boldface or all caps and follows it with **The Solution** or THE ANSWER. Both problem and solution are presented in the absolute minimum number of words — often no more than twenty.

The format used in the "Top Shop Tip" department of *Wood* magazine is typical of the illustrated tips used by publications for hobbyists and do-it-yourselfers. In this format, the problem is presented in italics or boldface type. It is followed by a drawing or photo to amplify the tip, which is printed below the illustration.

Whenever you study back issues of a magazine to determine format and content for your tips, take this hint to heart. Be sure the magazine copies are current. For example, only a few years ago, a popular *Better Homes and Gardens* department called "Tips, Tools and Techniques," used the Problem/Solution format. That department no longer exists. Instead, the current *BH&G* hints/tips department, "Family Network," emphasizes people-oriented problems and the advice is written in the form of letters.

The request for material at the end of the department says, "Family Network welcomes letters describing how you solved problems involving your family or your community, or letters asking for help with an unsolved problem."

One month's department, for example, consisted of nine letters with suggestions from readers in answer to the letter that prompted the greatest response the column so far has received (more than six hundred submissions). The letter sought advice on how to deal with a neighbor who replaces borrowed items with cheaper brands.

Another issue included six letters with tips on everything from cleaning a Little League ballpark to getting kids to turn off the lights. The seventh letter was a plea for advice from a twelve-year-old boy who would like to feel more comfortable around his relatives.

LOOKING BEYOND FORM TO SUBSTANCE

More important than the proper format is the material itself. Tips that are appropriate for some magazines just won't do for others. Any astute 30-Minute Writer will figure out by reading back issues of the magazine that *Friendly Exchange* is a travel magazine; it uses household-oriented hints only if they have been adapted to travel or camping.

Another publication that uses travel tips exclusively is *Adventure Road*. While many of the tips apply only to driving, such as keeping carpet samples in the trunk so you can slip them under your tires to get traction, others are adaptations of hints for everyday living.

Techniques you use to keep the youngsters occupied while you're driving around town might work equally well when applied to vacation driving; gas station time-savers you incorporate into your weekly routine could work equally well on the road.

FineScale Modeler prints model building hints in its "Tips and Techniques" department. *Home Mechanix* uses illustrated tips on projects around the house. *Parents Magazine* goes for tips on—as you might imagine—parenting. It would be a very unusual suggestion that would work for all three markets. The only one I can think of that could conceivably fit would involve construction of an area in your home where parents and children could work on model building together—a tall order for a short item.

This trend toward specialized hints and tips promises to continue. With the increasing efforts by publishers to make the personalities of specialty magazines more unlike their competitors, we can expect hints and tips, also, to become less look-alike.

Each magazine that uses hints and tips chooses them carefully so that they mesh not only with its readers' interests, but also with their life-styles, educational and financial levels and degree of sophistication.

You can get a lot of this information by reading the magazines and looking at their ads. The fact that *Modern Romances'* "Household How-Tos" and *True Experience's* "House Wise" focus on tips that make life around the house easier is only half the story. You'll also want to make the tips relevant to the lives of the people who read the magazines.

According to the listing in *Writer's Market*, *Modern Romances* is a "monthly magazine for blue-collar, family-oriented women, ages 18-65 years." *True Experience*, you'll find by looking at the masthead, shares the same publisher. By reading the magazine, you'll deduce that the readership, also, is similar.

Be aware, too, that tips that worked ten years ago won't generally sell today unless they're updated. Life-styles have changed so drastically that advice that's not current sounds naive at best. Any tip that assumes women have entire days to spend at home isn't realistic in today's world. Hints that apply only to the traditional two-parent family won't make it at a lot of publications, either.

Even money is regarded differently by today's thirty-year-olds than by their parents. And those thirty-year-olds regard it differently than they did before the economic cartwheels of the 1980s.

Granted, some publications are far more conservative than others. Most of their readers are living lives we used to think of as traditional. But even those readers have changed.

Television, with its fantasy-world entertainment and ads, its true-life battle scenes and matter-of-fact discussions of subjects that a quarter-century ago were considered inappropriate, has altered the expectations, perceptions and opinions of even the most tradition-bound among us.

These changes, added to each magazine's quest to be different from the others, have affected the short items like hints and tips as much as any part of the publication.

By way of illustration, let's look at *Woman's Day* and *Family Circle*. A decade ago, the tips in the "Neighbors" department of *Woman's Day* were virtually interchangeable with those in *Family Circle's* "Readers' Idea Exchange." They suggested clever ways of doing things and solving problems usually considered as "women's jobs."

Changing with the times, *Woman's Day* still has its "Neighbors" but the content has changed to focus almost entirely on relationships, the environment, and improving the lives of loved ones; how to keep love alive while working different hours; what to do to enrich family reunions; how to recycle plastic bags over and over before they go to the recycle bins. Items are somewhat longer than they used to be, too. The small print at the bottom of the page now says, "Do you have a true experience to contribute to Neighbors? . . . We'll pay $75 for each letter we publish."

The household hints, which formerly were incorporated into the "Neighbors" page, now appear in another department called "Mary Ellen Says." The magazine also pays seventy-five dollars for each of these that is printed. While there are about five or six "Neighbors" items (usually 75 to 100 words) purchased for each issue, twice as many tips (they can't exceed 50 words) are bought for the "Mary Ellen Says" page.

On the other hand, *Family Circle*, while changing the name of "Readers' Idea Exchange" to "Between Friends," still concentrates on household/child-oriented hints. These tips are generally shorter than those used ten years ago and seem more innovative. At one hundred dollars, they're also the best-paying per word, especially for those tips that are only 25 or 30 words long.

HINTS ON TIPPING THE SALES SCALES IN YOUR FAVOR

In many publications, each tip has a title, usually two to four words: "Child's Play," "Picture Perfect," "Soup's On." If your target magazine uses titles, include them with your submissions. They may take more effort to craft than the hints themselves but will be worth every minute of time spent. An eye-catching, "just right" title will distinguish your piece from the hundreds of others.

Pay close attention to the length of previously published tips. The hints in *Woman's World* usually consist of no more than 25 words. Often written in only one sentence, they're almost never longer than three: "Fix small scratches by rubbing walnut meat into them or by using a matching crayon to fill them in"; "Steady a wobbly table or chair by gluing a button under the short leg."

No matter what the length, hints and tips waste no words. After you've written yours, go over each of them, asking yourself which material is absolutely essential and deleting the rest.

KEEPING IN CIRCULATION

A time-efficient procedure for keeping track of your submissions is to list each of them on a separate file card by title (or using key words) along with as many potential markets as you can think of.

Along with each submission, be sure to include a self-addressed stamped envelope. Though some magazines inform contributors on their hints pages that no material will be returned, it will usually be sent back when rejected if an SASE has accompanied it.

How long should you wait before you submit your hint elsewhere? That's hard to answer since some editors say they have used items many months—and even years—after they were received. My advice is to write to the editor when you haven't heard anything on the status of your tip six months after you've submitted it, especially if you have alternate markets in mind. If the editor doesn't respond to your inquiry, go ahead and submit the idea to another suitable market.

You'll give your seasonal hints a better chance of seeing publication if you submit them six to eight months ahead of the appropriate season. Surprisingly, people send Christmas ideas to magazines when the December issues are already on their way to the newsstands.

If you have a choice of markets, start with the best-paying publications and work your way down. The highest rates I've seen are paid by *Family Circle*; *Woman's Day*, *Parents Magazine* and *Better Homes and Gardens* pay well, too, considering the small amount of time and energy you'll have to expend. Your chances will be best, however, with publications where the competition isn't so intense.

A logical extension of hints/tips writing is the short how-to article. You'll find these pieces in publications ranging from *Postcard Collector* and *Professional Quilter* to *1,001 Home Ideas* and *Mother Earth News*.

Though they generally run from 500 to 800 words, in some publications these mini-how-tos are no longer than 150 to 200 words and are essentially a series of tips on the solution of a problem or the execution of a project.

The tips are usually prefaced with one or two summarizing paragraphs, then listed in sequential order in the case of a project or in a progression appropriate to the solution of a problem. In some cases, the tips aren't dependent upon a particular order and so are best arranged to make the article read easily. Numbers, bullets or italicized first words are often used to set each point apart from the others.

Using a variety of the sentence starters discussed earlier, get quickly into your subject. Pack as much information as possible into each punchy paragraph. Active verbs and clear communication will give your piece a fast-paced, easy-to-read style that will help make your short tips salable.

THE 30-MINUTE WRITER'S PLAN OF ACTION

1. Gather together copies of as many magazines that use hints and tips as you can (or photocopy the hints and tips pages along with the publications' mastheads so that you have all the names and addresses you'll need for submitting).

2. Go on walkabout around your house and office, pen and paper in hand. Make lists of innovations you've dreamed up, problems you have solved. List, too, any problems you've heard friends or co-workers mention and try to figure out solutions.

3. Put your tips into the appropriate magazines' preferred

formats and send them off. Enclose an SASE if you want to get rejected ideas back so you can submit them to other publications. Even when editors say they don't return submissions, the SASE often prods them to do so.

CHAPTER VIII

Positively Inspirational

I don't know about you, but I like to get inspired. Not that a lot of action results from that inspiration, but reading positive-focus articles make us all feel good. Brightens our days.

We read about the abandoned kid in Glasgow who grew up to become a tycoon/philanthropist; about the effect positive thinking had on a group of Indianapolis secretaries; about the fry cook who befriends potential delinquents and turns them around. And we vicariously glow. The world isn't such a bad place after all.

Brighteners are the balancers, the antidote to all the stories about fraud, murder and mayhem. They're articles — usually a few paragraphs to a page or so in length — that focus on the positive. Some of them have a religious or philosophical theme; others tell about good things that have happened. All of them give us hope and happy feelings.

Like the op-ed and personal experience pieces, the brightener relies much more heavily on rolling thoughts around in your mind than it does on research. Because many of these articles come wholly from our own experiences and those of people close to us, they often only require our telling the story. It's also important to spend a large portion of the total time required thinking of appropriate subjects and finding fresh approaches to subjects that have been written about so often they can become clichés.

You can write successful one-page articles on just about any subject (provided you adjust the breadth of focus to the article length). But the success of your brighteners will depend in large part on the topics you have chosen.

Since brighteners (which also may be called inspirationals) take more thinking than research and writing time, they're projects that 30-Minute Writers might well consider, but only if those writers are upbeat, optimistic, and have faith that people are essentially good, that things happen for a purpose. Writers who genuinely believe that humankind is basically rotten won't be very convincing when they try to spread hope and good cheer.

An essential part of most brighteners is that they involve people, animals or other living things. But I've seen brighteners — and I am sure you have, too — woven around the certainty of the seasons, the glories of nature, faith in a supreme being.

The best-selling brighteners can be categorized in three groups: 1.) articles that make us happy by telling of good works and triumphs over adversity; 2.) pieces that help us cope with life through inspiration; and 3.) uplifting inspirationals that extol the wonders of creation.

Although religious faith plays an important role in the lives of many people who write brighteners, it certainly isn't essential. Some of the most upbeat, uplifting people I've known are agnostics, existentialists and atheists, capable of writing about all sorts of inspirational subjects.

Themes that predominate in the *good works/triumphs over adversity* articles are:

1. Helping hands
2. Be the best of whatever you are
3. Supreme determination despite horrendous odds/setbacks

They almost always involve people — individuals, groups with a common purpose or whole communities. The individual might be a grandmother who won't give up trying to find homes for "unadoptable" children even though she's confined to a wheelchair or the father who's determined that his mentally impaired son will play baseball. It might be the young man who, though profoundly disabled in an accident, beats the odds and learns to walk again.

The inspiring group may be people who tear down old houses and use the components to repair homes of the less fortunate in their small Louisiana village. Or they might be a handful of mothers in Harlem who drive drug dealers from their neighborhood.

Communities do all sorts of inspiring things. They save historical buildings condemned to the wrecking ball, inaugurate programs to feed the homeless, recycle discards and use the proceeds to plant trees, create free after-school programs for latchkey kids.

Occasionally, an individual, group and/or community may all be involved in a single article. Take the case of how the residents of my own community of Reno and the surrounding area were all affected by one person.

In 1990, Reno TV stations began covering the story of a local high schooler named Ryan Maloy, who had only a short time to live without a heart transplant. Ryan lived with his mother and two siblings. The family was on welfare.

The community rallied around and established a fund under the sponsorship of the Lions Club; Ryan became a star on the nightly news. Although his life was in jeopardy, he spoke in interviews about other area children with life-threatening problems and asked that the community help them, too.

Ryan's body ultimately rejected his new heart and he died. But tens of thousands of people in the community mourned his death and continue contributing to the fund he initiated.

You may find a triumph over adversity article that focuses on the deeds of an animal—the chimp that allows a paraplegic to live independently by helping with necessary tasks, the dog that has thwarted seven burglaries at a convenience store.

Themes for the *coping through inspiration* pieces run the gamut of all the commonly accepted virtues: forgiveness, truth, honesty, faith, love.

You can write about graceful acceptance, true contentment, thankfulness, putting yourself in another's place. You might use the theme of "don't give up" or "learn from adversity." In fact, you can write about almost anything that will make your readers think positively, that will help them psychologically and/or spiritually.

By showing those readers, for example, how you or someone else faced some problem or dilemma, you provide them with confidence to solve their own problems.

Uplifting inspirationals deal more with natural science than they do with human nature. The miracle of daffodils and hyacinths emerging from dead-looking bulbs; the magic of watching a blue heron standing by a lake at sunset; the serenity of a mountain meadow at dawn—anything about life that evokes a sense of wonder or awe can be used as the centerpiece of these brighteners.

IDEAL IDEAS

While you're becoming familiar with the various forms inspirationals/brighteners take, you are probably also getting ideas about themes/subjects you might write about.

Whenever you get one of these inspirations, I urge, beg and plead with you to write it down. Because our brains are so busy, ideas are regular Houdinis when it comes to escaping. A notebook especially for writing—one that fits in pocket or purse—works best for me.

Idea sources are all around us. We read newspaper accounts and magazine articles, have conversations with friends and family that (sometimes inexplicably) bring to mind situations, examples or themes that could fit into pieces that inspire.

Parallel ideas jump from the pages. We read a brightener about a retired businessman who helps single parents set up at-home businesses and we think of other retirees whose good works we know or have heard about. An article about the joy of walking through new-fallen snow starts us thinking about the satisfaction that comes from harvesting our gardens' bounty, the delight of watching spring buds unfold or of hiking new trails.

Some of the ideas may have been done to death. However, they can be resurrected with an approach that will lift them out of cliché territory. Instead of the predictable "hiking along new trails—new beginnings" connection, we might ultimately decide on walking along an old path and seeing it with new eyes, then enlarging the theme to one of looking at life not only from our old perspectives but also from the perspective of changing times.

To take ideas out of the cliché category, examine them with imagination. Change a single word in your premise, or add one, and you can come up with a completely different angle. For example, the joy of helping others can be transformed into helping the helpless help others, the basis for an article that tells about a program in which people with severe physical and/or mental challenges take part in projects that serve others' needs.

INSPIRATIONAL UNDERPINNINGS

The two essential ingredients of the brightener/inspirational are the vehicle and the theme. In the *good works/triumphs over adversity* themes, the vehicles are the individuals involved as well as the situations they battle against. The primary job of the writer is to find the story idea, then tell the story. Research will be minimal. Perhaps a few interviews will be necessary, and you may have to check some facts.

The *coping through inspiration* pieces involve a more complex—though not necessarily more difficult—construction.

You may choose a theme first, or you may start out by thinking of one of life's incidents that could be used in some way to teach a lesson or illustrate some positive point.

The easiest method is to think of an incident that would lend itself to dramatization and then decide which theme it best exemplifies. Perhaps the shabbily dressed woman ahead of you in the supermarket line asks the checker to return one of the items in her shopping basket to stock since she hasn't enough money to pay for it. Then, that same woman puts the quarter she receives in change into a "Help Feed the Hungry" container on the counter before she goes out with her bag of groceries. It doesn't take long for the writer of brighteners/inspirationals to realize that the incident provides a vehicle that illustrates charity in a way that works in well with the biblical Widow's Mite story.

Although it can be more difficult, you can go about the process by first defining your theme. Let's say that you want to write a piece about some special day of the year. You might choose the theme of leaving the past behind—it's an especially good one for Easter. Or you might want to write about forgiveness, since it's an appropriate theme for the beginning of a new year or for Yom Kippur.

Before you decide what to write about, however, you have to come up with material to support your theme. Do you have a powerful or dramatic or moving story to illustrate the point you want to make? Have people said meaningful things about your subject? Can you think of appropriate analogies that you might use?

Answer these questions by going over events in your past for illustrative stories, by looking through books of quotations to see what has been said that pertains to your theme, and by making a list of analogous thoughts.

Having grown up in a small town during the Great Depression with a wealth of stories handed down by my parents and relatives, I have an inventory of true-life incidents so vast that many of them will never be used. You most likely do, too, even if you were born in a great metropolis during times of plenty.

As far as quotes are concerned, you'll find that everyone from the Greek philosophers to present-day comedians has had something to say about such topics as peace, hardship and joy. In addition to being of use in your articles, these quotes are great prods to get you thinking, to make you investigate your own beliefs and attitudes.

Coming up with analogies isn't easy for everyone, but lots of writers find the mental gymnastics exciting. One of my former students, a natural at writing brighteners, used analogy to good effect in the first piece she submitted (and sold).

June began her article by telling about sourdough bread starter she had received from a friend, with instructions that after she had made her dough from the starter, she must save a bit of it to pass on to someone else. Then her article went on to liken the starter to love and how it, too, must be given away.

There were several reasons for June's success. First of all, she really enjoyed reading uplifting prose. In fact, she preferred it to other forms. Therefore, even before she began writing articles, she had an understanding of a variety of markets and their requirements.

Second, she was involved with friends who spent a great deal of their time helping others. That meant she had a pool of potential ideas on tap.

Finally, she knew instinctively what other readers would like to read about and she knew the brightener lingo so that she could work out themes that were winners and say what she wanted with exactly the right words.

Uplifting inspirationals almost all revolve around the theme of "Look around you at all the beauties/marvels nature has bestowed upon us to enjoy, and think about the meaning of it all." It naturally follows that the vehicle is some aspect of nature's wonder. The primary pitfall for people who want to write this type of brightener is the cliché, both as far as idea and words are concerned.

Consider the "breathtaking sunset," for instance. The idea is about as clichéd as you can find, yet good brightener writers continually find new ways to focus when they choose it as their vehicle. We have all read "breathtaking sunset" pieces and will most likely see them in the future. But each of them has a different approach.

Perhaps the writer's point is that a gorgeous sunset can follow the most dismal of days. Or it might be that no matter how many sunsets you've seen, each one is somehow different from the other and brings joy to the beholder.

As far as clichéd words and phrases are concerned, the successful writer, instead of writing about a "breathtaking sunset," shows the reader why it is. Perhaps because one night it appears as a thin red rim around the sun; on another, it looks like a watercolor of lavender, orchid and flaming pink.

FINDING YOUR INSPIRATIONAL VOICE

The articles can be written in anecdotal form, as profiles, essays or factual accounts. The *good works/triumphs over adversity* may be written either in first or third person. When written in first person, they are usually in the form of the author relating personal experiences. When in third, they're often accounts—generally chronological—of a problem/situation and how it was addressed by the individual, group or community.

The *coping through inspiration* pieces are written in first, second or third person. But whatever form they take, these pieces show, rather than tell, since the salable brightener/inspirational must never preach. It cannot be a sermon if it is to succeed.

Uplifting inspirationals often begin in the first person, then after a paragraph or two, switch to third person. Many of them, however, are written in third person throughout the piece.

You will learn that negative situations are almost always showcased at the beginning of the first two categories of these very positive pieces. There has to be a problem to have a solution.

A contaminated water supply that government officials won't acknowledge, an extremely high teenage suicide rate, AIDS-infected children in Hungarian orphanages, all are problems that people have tackled with inspirational results.

Unresolved guilt over words spoken in anger, shame for having acted unwisely, despair over being unable to conquer a shortcoming are only a few of the aspects of the human condition that can be addressed in *coping by inspiration* pieces.

In the course of your article analysis, pay attention to the number of difficult words that are used in a particular publication's inspirational pieces. Many of them are very simply written.

This means that crafting salable brighteners/inspirationals is relatively easy. The material for *good works/triumphs over adversity* articles is often so dramatic that you only need narrate the events as they occurred. When you choose this format, however, it's imperative that you develop a chronology the reader will find easy to follow.

To increase reader involvement, fictional techniques are often used. They're especially effective when used to describe a person or persons, to set up a dramatic scene or incident (the atmosphere in the operating room was tense as the doctors huddled around a tiny, silent newborn), or to relate case histories.

Another popular technique guaranteed to arouse reader interest is comparison/contrast:

> Linda Stephens is blonde, good looking and dresses in the latest fashions. Patti Carrigan is 100 pounds overweight and, although she is 18 years old, has to wear clothes that would be considered dowdy by women three times her age.

When this technique is used, the comparison/contrast is followed by an explanation telling why two people (or things) that are so dissimilar have some sort of relationship. In the case of the above example, the next paragraph might read:

> Yet the two women have become the best of friends through a program that pairs up successful "losers" with people who are struggling to take off weight — the brainchild of another woman who had to lose weight or die.

With those two paragraphs we have set the stage for an inspirational piece about a woman who devotes her time — without pay — to helping people whose excess weight is life threatening.

Coping through inspiration pieces — again using fiction techniques — commonly begin with a dramatization of the problem; for example, "It was a gloomy Saturday afternoon. The children had gone ice skating. My husband was watching a college football game on TV. I sat alone in my bedroom, wondering how I would find the emotional strength to get through another day."

Amplification of the problem follows next, after which (still in the storytelling mode) the writer goes on to describe whatever occurs that helps solve the problem. Don't complicate your writing life by telling of two dissimilar problems unless the solution is the same for both of them.

Uplifting inspirationals generally are highly descriptive. The meadow in bloom, the rainbow at the end of the storm — whatever aspect of creation you've chosen as your vehicle needs a fresh treatment to make the piece a success.

Since most brighteners/inspirationals are less than 1,000 words, the body of the piece must stay sharply focused, keeping all information relevant to your central idea. You may be writing about two men who spend their spare time scavenging old bicycles and parts, which they renovate for needy children. It's okay to mention that one of the men is a dentist and the other is a fast-food franchisee, but don't go into detail as to what part of dentistry the first man likes best or where the second man got his business experience unless it's necessary to the focus of your piece.

The conclusion of the *good works/triumphs over adversity* article may end with the natural end of the story: the man who vowed to walk again taking his first steps; the mothers' fight against street corner drug sales resulting in an 85 percent decrease in activity in their neighborhood; and so on.

Often, the final words of inspiration are in the form of a quote from one of the central characters in the story, such as, "As long as there are homeless people on the streets of Seattle, I will never give up trying to help them."

Coping through inspiration pieces usually end by pointing out or illustrating in some way that you have been (or have seen others who were) successful and want to help readers to succeed as well.

Uplifting inspirationals commonly come to their conclusions with a summarizing statement of the theme, such as "After the sun had faded, I realized that the frustrations of the day had begun to fade as well and that along with a new dawn tomorrow would come a new chance at changing my life."

Whatever its form, the conclusion leaves the reader with positive feelings: belief that the world isn't so bad after all; inspiration as to good works they might do to help others; hope that they, too, might be able to solve what seem like insurmountable problems.

WHAT DO YOU CALL IT?

Titles of brighteners/inspirationals may not all be the same length, but whatever publication they appear in, they have one characteristic in common. Almost all of them are labels, groups of words that have something to do with the content of the piece. "The Prisoner's Palm Sunday," "Our Perfect Celebration Place" and "Two Lost Boys" are examples of label titles that give readers a clue as to what the article is going to be about.

But whereas successful articles of all other kinds have titles that don't leave the reader guessing, you'll often find a brightener/inspirational title that's obscure.

"His Mysterious Ways" is a cliché title you'll find often enough to recognize the piece as being about some happening attributed to God, but labels like "Six Minutes of Awe," "Twice Blessed" and "The Choice" don't give the reader much of a hint.

TAKING EXCEPTION

Every once in awhile, you'll come upon an article that, while it can't be categorized exactly as inspirational, nonetheless inspires the reader. Examples that come immediately to my mind are the back pagers in *McCall*'s "Living Beautifully" department. They're all written by the same person, interior designer/author Alexandra Stoddard, which means they don't provide freelance opportunities.

What they do provide, however, are excellent examples of taking a theme—in this case, one's life-style—and developing a combination personal essay/how-to that inspires the reader. According to what we observe in contemporary magazines, this trend toward the hybridized inspirational/brightener promises to gain in popularity during the next decade.

Among the variations on her theme that Stoddard has used to good advantage are "The Home that Tells Who *You* Are," "Christmas Details that Make a Difference" (details that will be treasured most come from your heart) and "Reaching Out to Others."

The latter piece is composed of four anecdotes concerning the author's interaction with others, all amplifying the article's first paragraph:

We make a conscious choice to connect with someone else.

Usually making the connection requires action on our part. Merely thinking about it won't do.

Following the anecdotes, she ties them together with a summarizing paragraph:

. . . When we act on our instincts to see a friend or have a party or give someone we love something of ours, we feel a surge of energy. We learn more about ourselves and widen the dimension of our lives.

OUTLETS FOR YOUR INSPIRATIONAL ENERGIES

It's a common assumption that all of the religious magazines are natural markets for inspirational articles. Paging through *Writer's Market*, however, shows that only about half of the listings in the Religious section use inspirational pieces.

You'll find additional church-oriented markets by visiting bookstores that specialize in religious materials. While some of them do not carry magazines, others have several titles in their racks, including several aimed at Christian women that include a great proportion of inspirational material.

Don't forget that many religious publications are subscription only and won't be found on any newsstands. I have had great success in obtaining these hard-to-come-by magazines from the free magazine tables at the libraries in our area and from friends of different religious faiths who receive them in the mail.

Secular women's magazines are the other major market for inspirationals. You'll also come upon them in *Reader's Digest* and in newspaper Sunday magazines.

After you've identified markets looking for brighteners, send for their writers' guidelines and sample copies of the magazines if you don't already have them.

The guidelines will not only tell you about required word lengths and rates of payment, they'll often include information on desired content and style. For example, the *Country Woman* writers' guidelines say:

> *Inspirational* . . . material should reflect the positive way in which the country enhances your own life. Many of these pieces appear as seasonal "thoughts from the country" on the back cover or as a longer, reflective piece called "Reflections." Length: 500-750 words. Rate: $50-$75.

After you've collected a number of magazines with sales potential, read them carefully. By studying the articles editors have bought in the past, you will learn how to tailor your material to fit the publication. This is most visibly obvious in regard to length. Some brighteners are only a couple of paragraphs long; others, a page or more.

You will find in your analysis that some publications use only one type of brightener — for example, first person accounts of lessons learned that brought the author an awareness that helps him or her cope with life. Some editors buy only uplifting inspirationals written in third person; others are seemingly more interested in content than any particular form.

Subject matter, as illustrated above in *Country Woman*'s guidelines, can be tied to the magazine's focus. Sometimes, as in the case of *Annals of Sainte Anne de Beaupre*, the focus is a very specific one. The information in its listing in *Writer's Market* says, "Our aim is to promote devotion to St. Anne and Christian family values." Upon reading the magazine, you'll realize that no matter how inspiring your piece that shows how your faith in St. Catherine or St. Agnes brought you through a horrendous crisis, *Annals of Sainte Anne de Beaupre* won't be a suitable market.

When you're studying a specific publication, take into account the degree of religious or secular orientation. Brighteners/inspirationals, while often carrying a message that's religious in nature, don't necessarily have to do with God, Jesus or other figures considered by their followers to be divine.

If the magazine is put out by a specific religious denomination, be sensitive to the denomination-oriented words that are used. Try to zero in on the religion's philosophy, too.

Also be aware that editors of religious magazines do buy pieces that have nothing to do with religion. Many of them buy inspirationals that are strictly secular, that will be meaningful to readers regardless of their philosophical beliefs.

Check the degree of religiosity in secular magazine inspirationals as well and you'll realize that they often mention God or at least allude to deity.

I've perhaps belabored this point of religious persuasion. But it is very important, since a large number of inspirationals do have some degree of spiritual orientation. Many people become extremely emotional on the subject of religious beliefs and the last thing editors want to do is to alienate those readers who do. That means no sale if you haven't done your homework.

If you *do* pay attention to details, however, you'll be far more likely to find your days are brightened by accepted manuscripts.

WHO INSPIRES THE INSPIRER?

As with any other form of writing, even the most inspired writer will run out of good brightener ideas every so often. That's a signal to take a week or two of those precious thirty-minute segments in our lives and use them to recharge our emotional-psychological batteries.

Take a walk through the woods, skip stones on a pond, read a favorite play, look at the beautiful colors of skeins in a yarn shop. Sit on a bench at the mall and people-watch. Stroll along a seaside pier or an amusement park midway, absorbing the sights, sounds and smells. Expose yourself to aspects of life with which you've grown out of touch. Let serendipity take over.

As Alexandra Stoddard wrote in one of her "Living Beautifully" pieces, appropriately titled "Get Inspired!":

> Caught up in our daily routines, the comfortable scenes of our lives dulled by familiarity, we need to remember the power of inspiration and open ourselves to its possibilities. Inspiration comes in

serendipitous ways, but it is always a gift, one that stimulates our faculties, fuels our creativity and, invariably, moves us to positive action.

THE 30-MINUTE WRITER'S PLAN OF ACTION

1. Start a "brighteners" file of the inspirational articles that appeal to you most. Categorize them as to type: good works/triumphs over adversity, coping with life through inspiration and uplifting inspirationals.

2. Assign different pages in your notebook to potential themes you might use. Under each theme, write ideas that amplify it, including words that will trigger your memory regarding anecdotes and experiences.

3. When you have spare minutes, take those anecdotes, experiences and descriptions and rough them out on paper. This work will serve two purposes: It will prime the idea-generating part of your brain and give you a head start when you need to turn those rough drafts into polished anecdotes to illustrate your inspirational articles.

4. If your articles involve interviews, schedule them for times when you won't feel rushed. Inspirational people are often *so* inspirational that you'll get the information you need plus a host of other uplifting ideas. Given the time, they'll also refer you to other inspirational people.

5. Decide on two themes and begin rough drafting your articles, always using previously published inspirationals in your target magazine as structural patterns. The reason I suggest working on two pieces simultaneously is that when you bog down on one of them, you can turn your writing attention to the other. It takes more of your precious thirty-minute sessions to write two pieces. But when you're dealing with articles that require great doses of mental energy, most people burn out less easily if they switch writing projects occasionally.

6. Set your rough drafts aside for a few days. Then examine them with fresh eyes. How's the continuity? Does the piece flow or does it bump along awkwardly? Usually, problems in this area occur when you need more material on a subject, perhaps a second illustration or a quote. Try rearranging paragraphs. Sharpen sentences to say exactly what you want them to. Scrutinize your adjectives to be certain they're apt. Throw out any clichés that might have crept into your work.

7. Send your manuscripts—neat and unsmudged—to the editors you've decided will be most inspired.

CHAPTER IX

Dining for Dollars

Whenever I hear of struggling writers who live in garrets and warm their soup over cans of Sterno, I shake my head in dismay. Why in the name of Craig Claiborne aren't they dining on nectar and ambrosia at that charming cafe two blocks down the street and writing a review about it?

One writer, Karen MacNeil, did just that. "I was renting in a poor Puerto Rican neighborhood—the ghettoey area of Manhattan," says MacNeil. "I saw an ad in the paper for a restaurant reviewer. I decided to apply: It was solely to eat."

The editor was discouraging. Why should he hire her when many of the applicants were well-known reviewers, he asked. But MacNeil was hungry, so she talked him into giving her one day to prove herself.

Since MacNeil didn't have money to spare for dinner, she headed to the bar at her favorite restaurant for information.

After she had deluged the bartender with questions and requests for recipes, the chef came out of the kitchen. "But wait, Madam," he said. "Come in and have dinner."

"All kinds of dishes floated out of the kitchen," says MacNeil. "Some I'd never seen before. At 2 A.M., full and satisfied on the best meal of my life, I got home and wrote." She landed the job, and her career—which has included food-focused pieces for *Travel & Leisure*, *Bon Appetit* and *Food Arts Magazine* and a book on nutrition and cuisine—was launched. Now, she's one of the country's top food writers.

You don't have to be starving to become a restaurant reviewer. Any writer with a taste for good food can develop the skills necessary to sell culinary comments. And what a great time-saver for 30-Minute Writers. We have to eat anyway, so why not get paid while we're doing it!

Of course, it will also help if you're familiar with all kinds of foods and not timid about trying the unfamiliar. You should have (or acquire) a good knowledge of cooking techniques, too, so that you can tell whether the salmon was poached or sautéed, and have an idea of how the chef produced that delicious citron sauce. It's also important to keep abreast of food trends. I like to read magazines for food professionals as well as those of the consumer variety.

How do you acquire the necessary information when you're on a tight time budget? Fifteen minutes' worth here, half an hour's worth there. Substitute cookbooks for the novels you read on your commute, paying special attention to the general information sections on sauces, cooking methods and spices. Grab a food and drink magazine instead of *Time* or *Newsweek* while you're waiting to have your teeth cleaned. Take ten minutes to talk to the produce man at the supermarket, asking him to identify the fresh herbs or unusual mushrooms you might not have noticed before.

POSTGRADUATE GASTRONOMICS

In order to tell about your dining adventures, you have to know what exactly it is that you have eaten, so you'll want to invest in some cookbooks if you don't already have a lifetime supply. My reference library includes a battered copy of *Escoffier Cook Book*, the *New York Times*, *Gourmet* and *Silver Palate* cookbooks, Julia Child's *Mastering the Art of French Cooking*, and that marvelous kitchen standby, *The Joy of Cooking*, as well as an assortment of specialty cookbooks. I have four books on grilling and ethnic cookbooks galore.

I also buy paperbacks of restaurant reviews when I'm traveling and cut out the best of the magazine reviews for my files. My criteria for judging these reviews include satisfactory answers to the following questions:

1. Does the place or the food sound different/outstanding enough to provoke my interest?
2. Is the piece so smoothly put together that it reads effortlessly?
3. Has the writer been able to avoid cliché words and phrases ("sumptuous repast," "mouth-watering")?
4. Has the writer been able to convey a sense of the place and ambience as well as the appearance/textures/seasonings of the various dishes?
5. Does the review contain enough specific information to enable the reader to make an informed decision about going there?
6. Is my interest aroused or am I entertained?

You might want to start a review file, too, even before you start querying editors about the possibility of writing food pieces. The reviews will give you lots of hints about how to craft your own.

It will also help (and perhaps provide material for other articles) to take some gourmet cooking courses. Watch for those offered by kitchenware shops, utility companies and appliance stores, since they're often free. Saturday morning TV cooking shows can sometimes be of value, but usually the chefs spend so much time trying to be clever that your time is better spent watching cooking videos that you've rented or checked out of the library.

If you can, arrange to spend an hour or so in the kitchen of any good-sized restaurant, observing the chopping, stirring, saucing and garnishing. I've gained access to restaurant kitchens in a variety of ways: by expressing my interest to restaurant managers; by interviewing chefs and then asking if I can watch them at work; via friends of friends who own restaurants and intercede on my behalf. It's also fairly easy to arrange a visit to the kitchen of a restaurant you've reviewed in the past.

Read books about foods and wine. They are great bedtime reading and will add to your body of culinary knowledge. The more you know about food preparation, the better reviews you will write.

PLEASING THE PUBLISHER'S PALATE

Knowing your onions and being able to write entertainingly won't automatically make you into a successful restaurant reviewer. You'll also need to sharpen your marketing skills, for even the best-crafted review doesn't have a chance unless it's paired with the right publication.

In addition to the many newspapers that feature food and restaurant reviews, there are a variety of magazines that print them regularly. You'll want to become familiar with as many of them as you can.

City and regional magazines are where you'll find the most opportunities. Some of them use reviews of single restaurants. Others like reviews that compare three or four of a particular kind of eatery—elegant cafes, pizza parlors, Thai restaurants or Mexican buffets, for instance. And still others want reviews about a half-dozen restaurants located in a particular area of the city or region covered by the magazine.

Since the offices of city and regional magazines are usually not too far from where you live, phone the editor for an appointment. Then, armed with a sample review (or clips of reviews you have published elsewhere), meet with her to talk about restaurants. Have several in mind and tell her about them. Even if your city or regional publication doesn't usually run restaurant reviews, your visit to the editor might prove productive. Perhaps she has considered them but hasn't yet found the person for the job. If she hasn't thought about using reviews, your conversation may prompt her to do so.

The most prestigious showcases for your restaurant reviewing talent are the food and drink magazines. However, they're also the markets where competition is toughest. When *Gourmet* or *Bon Appetit*, for example, use restaurant reviews, they're usually in the form of feature articles highlighting the cuisine of a city or area such as Brussels or the Basque country. Pay is at the top end of the scale, and chances for a newcomer to break into their pages are almost nil.

Airline in-flights are a more realistic market. Many of them use some form of review, either subjective or brief, objective pieces about dining places in their route cities.

Although auto club publications used to be good markets, too, most of those that now print information on restaurants use brief, staff-written descriptions of those that advertise in the publication.

And then there are newspapers. Their editorial offices are accessible to most of us and, although the pay isn't terrific, a good place to start since many of them don't have a sole writer doing all the restaurant copy.

An effective way to get a foot in the editorial door is by making an appointment with the editor of the Life-style section, proposing to review specific restaurants (have copies of their menus along, if possible), and leaving with the editor a package containing your résumé and copies of published reviews. If you haven't been published, do your best job of writing two or three reviews in proper manuscript form about local restaurants.

It's often difficult to tell by reading reviews whether they are written by freelancers, staffers or writers assigned to do them on a regular basis. The best way to find out is by making a twenty-second call to the publication's editorial offices.

At any time it's a good idea to query the editor, either by mail or in person, outlining the restaurants you wish to review (but adding that you're receptive to any suggestions he might have).

If you send a manuscript to any magazine without querying first, you run the risk of wasting postage on an idea that duplicates one already in the works or that doesn't jibe with the editor's plans.

When deciding which restaurants to query about, choose those that complement eating places featured by the publication in the past, whether sophisticated, family-style or funky. The restaurant should be worth reviewing; that is, it should serve well-prepared food and should not be on the verge of having its health department permit revoked. You'll get ideas about potential candidates from friends, ads in newspapers, phone books, local tourist publications, and your own dining experiences.

Through the years, I have had a variety of experiences—including food poisoning—connected with restaurant reviewing. Some of the pieces I've written have been about single restaurants; others, about several. One piece for a food and drink magazine, "Best Bets in Reno," was about posh dining spots just blocks from our home. Several for airline in-flights were about out-of-the-ordinary restaurants in or near their route cities.

Now, most of my restaurant reviews are for *Nevada* magazine. It's an ideal arrangement, since the magazine's editorial offices are less than a forty-five-minute drive away and I can reach the editor with a local phone call. Most of the restaurants I write about aren't far away, either, which is a real time-saver. Another advantage about writing up local restaurants is that you get lots of tips on good places to eat from friends, so basic research never takes very long. When I was assigned a piece on Reno's casino buffets, everyone I knew told me about their favorites—and volunteered to go along to help.

GETTING READY FOR DINNER

Your reviewing job will be easier if you devise a worksheet to take with you to the restaurant. You may feel conspicuous (not to mention gauche) taking notes in white-linen-and-candlelight establishments, but this problem can be solved by a couple of well-timed trips to the powder room for intensive scribbling.

In less elegant surroundings, I usually fold my review form (printed side out) in the pages of an oversize paperback. That way, from time to time I can open the book, jot down a phrase or two, and resume eating.

The form I've devised looks like this. I write additional comments on the reverse sides of each sheet, which are blank.

Name of Restaurant _____

Address _____

Phone Number _____ Hours Open _____
Days Closed _____
Credit Cards Accepted (Check Those Applicable)
     Visa ☐   MasterCard ☐   American Express ☐   Discover ☐
     Other_____

Decor/ambience (e.g., wall coverings, flocked wallpaper, photos of old lumber mills, cabinets of china and cut glass, piano player who does show tunes) _____
_____
_____
_____

Clientele (e.g., young professionals, dock workers) _____
_____
_____

Seating: tables, booths, banquettes, counters (e.g., color scheme and material used) _____
_____
_____

Table Settings: dishes, glassware, linen, place mats, flowers, or other decoration (e.g., What colors are they? What materials? Ironstone dishes, silk flowers?) _____
_____
_____

Waiter/waitress attire, if out of the ordinary (e.g., peasant blouses, black bodices and pastel dirndl skirts, artist's smocks and berets) _____
_____
_____

House specialties (brief description of each) _____
_____
_____
_____
_____

Special touches (e.g., individual loaves of bread, pots of pâté, fingerbowls, special menus for children, complimentary liqueurs, red roses presented to ladies on leaving) _____
_____
_____

Price range (specify whether complete dinner or à la carte) _____

_____

Wine list: examples and prices (e.g., extensive selection, rare vintages, wide assortment of California, French or German) _____

Bar/drink features (e.g., drinks garnished with paper umbrellas and fresh fruits, unusual glassware, exotic drinks) _____

_____

Highlights (e.g., dessert cart, singing waiters, excellent salads) _____

_____

Weaknesses (e.g., slow service, cold food, dishes too highly/lightly seasoned) _

_____

Additional Comments _____

_____

_____

READY, SET, EAT

I prefer to dine alone when I am reviewing. Distractions are minimal, I can take complete notes without being rushed, and there is plenty of room on the table for my book. Since it is not uncommon for business travelers to work while they're eating, taking notes usually doesn't attract attention. But even if servers catch on that you're writing a review — and if they're good servers they shouldn't have time to read your notes — it won't really matter as, although service may improve, the chef can't transform the quality of a meal on such short notice.

The advantage of group dining (being able to sample more of the menu choices) is outweighed for me by these considerations unless my dinner companions are gourmets who delight in spending the mealtime discussing the food.

If you're being paid well enough to afford it (or someone else is picking up the tab), visit the restaurant twice: the first time alone; the second, with one to three gourmet friends who will share their reactions and let you sample what they've ordered.

If your one-time experience at the restaurant is solo, order house specialties, including at least one item from each category of courses. Never order a food you detest. No matter how well it is prepared, odds are you won't like it.

When your meal is really bad, you might want to give the restaurant a second chance—if your wallet and stomach can absorb the cost. Perhaps it was the chef's night off, his stand-in got sick, and the cooking was done by the proprietor's two fifteen-year-old nieces. If a return visit is out of the question, try to learn whether the regular chef was in the kitchen or if there were other extenuating circumstances. When you can't find out, you might want to write something like, "It's possible that I was there on an off night" to be as fair as you can. Anyone who has ever cooked knows that there can be times when the mayonnaise curdles and the custard won't set. As a reviewer, you will want to be sure your evaluations are accurate.

AFTER-DINNER HINTS

Though I make it a practice to visit restaurant review candidates unannounced, as I leave I always present my card and request a copy of the menu (with a promise to return it). When, in the course of my reviewing, I plan to dine at a restaurant twice, I do this at the end of my second visit.

If necessary, I also make an appointment to interview the manager or owner within a day or two. These interviews are usually brief. During the fifteen or twenty minutes I allocate for this facet of my research, I find out who the owners are, how they got into the restaurant business, and when they began. I also obtain background information on the head chef and the manager: where they were trained, where they worked in the past. This is vital when you're writing a review for a publication whose past reviews have always included that information.

Occasionally, I also speak to the chef—to find out what he did to give the chocolate mousse such a flawless texture or what she put into the vichyssoise to achieve that distinctive flavor. Some reviews are accompanied by recipes, and the chef is the person to get them from (get the manager's permission to print the restaurant's recipes first).

PICKING UP THE TAB

How your dining costs will be paid depends upon the publication for which you're writing. Some magazines and most newspapers reimburse reviewers for costs (within limits). Other magazines — especially those with a tourism, public relations tie-in — obtain complimentary meals from the restaurants reviewed. Still others require that the writer pay. None of the three is "standard" practice, so it's best to inquire before you start making dinner arrangements. Since the pay for most restaurant reviews is at least seventy-five dollars (and often a good deal more), paying for your meals won't hurt so much.

In the invitation situation, the pros recommend that you present the invitation after you have finished the meal to insure that you'll get the same treatment your readers can expect.

Above all, when you're comped for a meal, be sure not to let that fact get in the way of your objectivity. Remember, your readers won't be comped; they will have worked to earn the money they're spending on your recommendation. A restaurant reviewer's first duty is to his or her readers, not to the restaurant.

SLAVING OVER A HOT WORD PROCESSOR

After you've read reams of restaurant reviews and have written a few of them, you'll acquire an extensive vocabulary of adjectives. If you have the foresight to include these key terms on the worksheet you use at the restaurant, you'll make the actual writing of the review much smoother. Noting the words that carry the exact nuances you wish to convey is especially important in restaurant reviewing. Take a *small* versus an *intimate* dining room, for example; or *attentive* versus *efficient* service. In each pair, one adjective conveys a meaning quite different from that of the other.

The reason for all these descriptive words is to give the reader a strong sense of ambience. Note the descriptive phrases in this short review by Randy Tindle of Yang Ming in Bryn Mawr, Pennsylvania, which appeared in the November, 1991, issue of *Delaware Valley*:

Yang Ming, on Conestoga Road in Bryn Mawr, Pennsylvania, where the old Conestoga Mill once stood, shatters the old Chinese restaurant shibboleth that the more attractive and relaxing the ambience, the more nondescript the food. We entered a brightly appointed cocktail area with a blond mahogany bar where a tuxedoed maitre d' greeted us cordially and quickly showed my lunch partner and me to a table. Tipping the maitre d' is not required, says the manager.

Entrées range from $9.95 to $19.95. We decided to split the seafood in a flower basket ($16.95) with steamed dumpling appetizers — one order stuffed with pork and vegetables ($5.50), the second stuffed with crabmeat ($6.95). The dough envelopes were delicate and juicy, suggesting that they had been mixed, Szechuan-style, in cabbage juice. The pork was delectable, with a slight bite; the crabmeat didn't taste precisely like crabmeat, but whatever they mixed with it gave it an agreeable pungency.

Our pièce de résistance — the seafood in a flower basket — was irresistible; generous chunks of lobster, scallops, jumbo shrimp and crabmeat sauteed in garlic and herbs served in a basket of deepfried noodles. It tasted just as fresh and firm as it looked.

Montgomery County's Yang Ming is located at 1051 Conestoga Road in Bryn Mawr, (215) 527-3200. It's open for lunch Monday — Saturday 11:30 a.m. — 3 p.m.; dinner Monday — Thursday 3 — 10 p.m., Friday — Saturday 3 — 11:30 p.m., Sunday 2 — 10 p.m. There is a full bar, and Visa, MasterCard and American Express are accepted. The restaurant is wheelchair accessible. Reservations are taken for parties of five or more only.

Reviews generally have information of the sort in the above paragraph either at their beginning or end, usually set off with italics or boldface. The reason is obvious: Readers who decide to act on the reviewer's recommendations can find such info as the restaurant's location, phone number and, sometimes, hours of operation easily, without having to wade through the text.

When you're writing your restaurant reports, be sure to put the nuts and bolts information into the form that the magazine has used in the past. It's attention to details like these (attention that really doesn't demand that much of your time) that whets an editor's appetite for your work.

COOKING UP GREAT REVIEWS

To my way of thinking, the best review writing is relaxed, with clever turns of phrase—a style popular with most editors. Ingrid Wilmot, who writes restaurant reviews for airline in-flights and regional magazines, is one of the best in the business. Her recipe for a well-crafted review includes "knowledge of preparation of food, fairness, an open mind, a curious palate, plus a touch of humor."

Paul Fischer, restaurant critic for *Boston Magazine*, used that touch of humor when starting out his review of area steakhouses titled "Here's the Beef" this way:

> The times I feel most American—as opposed to a walking, talking bowl of ethnic stew from the big melting pot—are when I order steak in a restaurant. More than ideology, the size of our nuclear arsenal, or even the Slinky, what really separates us Americans from everybody else in the world has always been a great T-bone steak.
>
> Oh, sure, everyone says that communism is disintegrating under populist demands for democracy, the so-called cornerstone of the American way. But while all those people in Poland and Hungary are shouting for free elections and multiparty systems and (cover your ears, Karl!) free markets, what they really want are Christmas bonuses and big fat juicy grilled steaks on the table— just like in the good old U.S. of A. The Eastern European masses

don't really want their own White House, they want porterhouse, with lots of mushrooms and onions.

As with other forms of writing, the recipe for a successful restaurant reviews must be adapted to fit the culinary requirements of the publication picking up the tab. But, whether the reviews are short ones like that of Yang Ming or long like "Here's the Beef" (it ran some 1,900 words), editors all like leads that are grabbers, that will intrigue their readers so that they'll go on to the finish.

APPETIZING OPENERS

The most popular leads are narrative (especially when the restaurant has a long and interesting history), summary, anecdotal, descriptive or a combination thereof. The two examples that follow will give you a sampling of what the editors of *In Paradise* and *Chicago* like.

The first, "Wo Fat," which appeared on the pages of *In Paradise*, is by Bob Norton.

There's no Mr. Wo, and no Mr. Fat at Wo Fat Restaurant in Honolulu. The word "Wo" means harmony or peace, while "Fat" denotes prosperity. The names were chosen by the restaurant's founders 108 years ago for their auspiciousness. And obviously chosen well, because in a town where nine out of 10 eateries belly up after three years of operation, and merely hanging on for five years automatically confers "landmark" status on any restaurant, Wo Fat Restaurant is nothing short of a living legend here in Honolulu and the Islands.

The second, "Class-A BBQ" in the Budget Beat section of *Chicago*'s "Dining" department, was written by Anne Spicelman and David Novick.

Many are moved to open rib shacks, but few have mastered the secrets of really dynamite barbecue. And although fired-up fans heatedly argue the merits of their favorites, only a handful of joints generally are acknowledged as Chicago treasures.

Nida's Old-World Narra Smokehouse (1513 West Irving Park Rd.) belongs among them. Larry Tucker's bare-bones spot with its look-of-log-cabin counter and seven tables is less than six months old, but the barbecue is the best we've had in years. Almost everything else on the compact menu is equally good, no mean achievement considering the eclectic line-up. It ranges from a Mediterranean salad with grilled chicken breast (perfect for cholesterol and calorie counters) to Filipino pancit noodles, a tribute to Tucker's fiancee, Nida Poso, who hails from the islands. Narra, by the way, is the Philippine hardwood Tucker's dad used for barbecuing during World War II.

I don't know about you, but these reviews tempt me to find out more about the restaurants the lead paragraphs introduce us to. And that's important, because the restaurant review's goal should be to inform (and sometimes entertain) the reader.

Editors have their preferences as to style and structure/organization of materials so it's necessary to read the publications you want to write for in order to determine what they are. However, most reviews follow a basic format.

After the lead, be it descriptive, anecdotal, narrative or a summarizing statement, the midsections of reviews contain the meat and potatoes (or the shish kebab and couscous, if you will). They tell about the decor, the ambience, and describe certain dishes that are on the menu. They may describe, too, how the people who wait on you are dressed and what kind of service you can expect. The middle paragraphs sometimes also contain information on the chef and/or other personnel and the owners. Quite often, one or more of these people will be quoted; for example, " 'People aren't out for flour and water; they want meat in their sausage,' Arv declares."

Remember that the primary focus of almost all restaurant reviews is on food and drink, but you have other aspects of the dining experience to cover as well, so balance is important. If you have a limit of 500 words, for example, you'll want to devote at least 150 to 200 of those words to the food and beverages served.

Winding up reviews is a snap when the magazine or newspaper format requires the service information at the end. If that material appears at the beginning of the publication's reviews, you'll need to come up with an ending; a brief statement that amplifies your theme, a quote, or a short anecdote are most often used.

A simple way to close is to keep reviewing food until the end. Norton's "Wo Fat" review did it like this:

> For decades, the all-time bestsellers at Wo Fat have been—and still are—the scallop soup, spicy Mongolian beef, honeymoon shrimp (seasoned shrimp speared with tender broccoli and pan-fried to perfection), Hong Kong-style chicken (juicy roasted chicken basted with a special sauce and served with condiment salt), authentic Peking duck, Canton chicken vegetable salad, honey-barbecued ribs and the best minute chicken cake noodles in all Hawaii—bar none!

The "Wo Fat" ending, while slightly more enthusiastic than most, isn't markedly so. You see, the majority of good restaurant critics—if given a choice of eating places—will review those they've heard good things about and anticipate will interest their readers.

For instance, Carol Cutler, author of eight food-focused books and numerous restaurant reviews, believes that the only time a negative review is called for is if "a great restaurant is slipping and you need to warn the reader." Otherwise, Cutler feels that the reviewer should seek out restaurants worthy of recommendation. "Negative reviews are easy to write," she says, "but what use are they to the reader?"

TRUTH IN RESTAURANT REVIEWING

Be aware of fair comment as it applies to press law. It's perfectly okay to criticize a restaurant's food, service and decor. But if you say that the place is a total loss, that its personnel are incapable of producing a decent meal or providing adequate service, you had better be prepared to appear in court.

The reviews I feel most comfortable writing are those about restaurants I have chosen myself. Eating out is expensive, and under no circumstances do I want to lead unsuspecting diners to the local ptomaine tavern or give a bum steer to a steakhouse. When I select my own review restaurants, I've exercised quality control even before I begin writing.

Anne Mackenzie, whose restaurant reviews have appeared in the Baltimore *News American*, *Maryland Magazine* and the Bel Air *Aegis*, likes to visit each restaurant twice in the company of her husband or a photographer, ordering the establishment's most requested dishes. Although Mackenzie believes that "a little constructive criticism" is part of the reviewer's job, she will never "truly pan" a restaurant, as she has seen a number of them fail as the result of a critic's comments. In addition to remarking on ambience, food, service and the wine list and giving particulars about location and such, Mackenzie suggests that writers also include information on what services for the handicapped are available.

But there are times when restaurant write-ups are assigned by editors of hotel in-room visitors' guides or magazines such as weekly tourist publications. These markets don't allow the reviewer the freedom to comment as candidly as non-public relations magazines do, since reviews are usually about restaurants that advertise in the publications.

City and regional magazines also may be unwilling to use reviews with much commentary that's negative. The reason is obvious. They don't want to lose the goodwill of current or prospective advertisers.

It is possible, however, to be honest without writing a negative word, especially if you're called upon to do a number of short reviews. Wax enthusiastic with mouth-watering adjectives about the eateries that are really memorable, and confine your remarks on the unrecommendables to "House specialties include . . . ," "Among the less expensive entrees are . . . ," or "A half dozen desserts are offered, including Jell-O, fruit cocktail and chocolate sundaes." First-rate reviewing, whatever form it takes, involves detouring readers away from the soggy soufflé as well as singing praise to the paella.

If the decor is tacky, you don't have to say so. Just describe it objectively. Readers will opt in most cases for the cafes you've written about in glowing terms, and you needn't worry about having led them astray. Beside, some people may like orange formica with cerise velvet drapes.

GARNISHING YOUR REVIEW

After you've finished your review, you come to the hard (or to some writers, the most exciting) part: cooking up a name for your piece. Some of the cleverest article titles I've seen were for restaurant reviews. One I especially like is "Ciao Down," about a place in Minneapolis that serves northern Italian food. Another good one is "No Fashion Plates, Please," about a no-pretenses restaurant in New Orleans.

Occasionally, but not often, you'll be asked to supply photos of the reviewed restaurant. Find out first whether the editor wants exterior or interior shots or both. Then see if the restaurant management has any shots on file. Check them out to determine whether they're of publishable quality.

If no photos are available, try to get the restaurant to hire a professional to take them. Point out that it will be to their advantage as great pictures have tremendous publicity value. As a last resort, take the photos yourself or find a freelance photographer friend to do it for you.

Taking photos of restaurant interiors is tough, unless you have professional models and proper lighting to work with, and photographing food is even more difficult. It's a job for a professional who specializes in that kind of photography, so avoid it if you can.

Don't be surprised if, after your byline appears regularly on restaurant reviews, you start receiving invitations to judge chili cook-offs, state fair cookie-baking contests and the like. For in writing, one experience always seems to lead to another.

Perhaps, like Karen MacNeil, you'll go on to books on nutrition and cuisine. Or you may become so *enormously* successful reviewing restaurants that you'll be able to write diet books with great authority.

THE 30-MINUTE WRITER'S PLAN OF ACTION

1. Write two or three reviews about interesting restaurants within the area your intended publication covers.

2. Make a list of half a dozen additional restaurants in the area that you think would make for good writes.

3. Either make an appointment and talk to the editor personally or send your reviews, the list, and a cover letter setting forth your interest and qualifications.

4. When assignments come, schedule your dining out evenings so that you won't be rushed or overly tired.

5. Tasting and observing are the most important things you'll be doing on the scene. You probably won't have time for really heavy eating or conversation.

6. Write the first draft of your review in segments—food, decor, setting and the like—perhaps just expanded versions of the notes you have written on the information form you took along. It's easier to integrate the information when you have it all down in rough form.

7. Look through your notes and memory for something unusual about the restaurant—something that sets it apart from the rest. A place's individuality usually lends itself to a strong lead.

8. Move the component parts around on your word processor (or cut and paste if you're typing) until you get a review that flows naturally.

9. If you find holes in the piece, phone the restaurant to obtain the material you need or make a return trip to look at it again.

CHAPTER X
Getting Personal

What I look upon as my all-time career high — as far as the ratio of time spent to satisfaction/payment received — is a piece called "Farewell to Sunday Best," which appeared in *Woman's Day* some years ago.

The idea came to me full blown and complete with lead paragraph. Then, minutes later, illustrative anecdotes popped into my mind like scenes from a movie. It was, I am quite certain, the only completely "top of my head" piece I have ever written.

The essay was about the folly of "saving things for good" rather than getting pleasure from using them. It evoked a great deal of response from readers. In their letters, they vowed that they were going to start wearing those brand-new shirts and ties and night-gowns that had reposed, gift-boxed, in their drawers for years; to set the table for family meals with the company china.

I don't expect, ever again, to write an article so easily. But I do hope to keep writing pieces that bring as much reader response. And the most likely way to do that is by coming up with more personal essays.

Though the personal essay is a lot like the op-ed piece, there are major differences. Both are usually no more than 1,000 words long, but whereas the op-ed is based upon opinions — which one hopes derive from logic — the personal essay springs from feelings.

The op-ed is almost always issue-oriented, while the personal essay often is not. In fact, the focus of personal essays can run the topical gamut from gun control to bubble gum, making this a much broader form. And while both types of pieces are often written in a combination of first and third person, the personal essay depends much more heavily upon the author's personal experiences and reactions to them. In op-eds, the writer can very well be uninvolved personally; he or she simply has a strong opinion on the subject.

Although their structures may be very much the same, the tone of the personal essay is almost always more relaxed, more conversational. And instead of the op-ed "this is how I believe it is and I'm going to do my best to convince you" tone, the personal essay derives its appeal from giving the reader a peek at some facet of the writer's life.

This is the reason personal essays fit so well into the 30-Minute Writer's life. We all have experiences that can be the basis for these "think" pieces. They rarely require much, if any, research, and can readily be put together bit by bit. They're the sort of articles that require lots of thinking, but it's usually the kind you can do while you're performing other tasks.

Another reason you should consider getting personal is that great motivator—demand. Since the trend toward personal essays is a strong one, each month a number of established magazines alter their formats (if they haven't yet done so) to include them. And new publications make their newsstand debuts each month, offering additional market potential.

You will notice that there's a certain amount of crossover as far as subject matter is concerned. Although politics, government and the law are far more popular as op-ed topics, certain other subjects such as abortion, child abuse and medical dilemmas have been written about extensively in both op-ed pieces and personal essays.

But observe the difference in the way those subjects are treated. In the op-ed, the writer takes a position and seeks to justify his/her stand with supporting evidence. In the personal essay, the writer makes the point by personalizing the subject.

Perhaps the most important difference between the two forms is this: Though the reader need not agree with the writer's point of view in the op-ed, the reader must identify — or, at least, empathize — with the writer's situation in order for the personal essay to succeed.

Of all the personal essays I have read, the one with which I identified most strongly was written by Alex Molnar and appeared in the *New York Times* on August 23, 1990. It was called "If My Marine Son Is Killed." Although the piece appeared on an editorial page and the format is unorthodox, the piece can definitely be classified as a personal essay. The following excerpts illustrate the writer's deep personal involvement.

Dear President Bush:
   I kissed my son goodbye today. He is a 21-year-old marine. You have ordered him to Saudi Arabia. . . .
   While visiting my son I had a chance to see him pack his chemical weapons suit and try on his body armor. I don't know if you've ever had this experience, Mr. President. I hope you never will. . . .

And the piece ends:

   If, as I expect, you eventually order American soldiers to attack Iraq; then it is God who will have to forgive you. I will not.

I realize that not everyone who read the piece had a son who was a Marine headed for the Persian Gulf, as we had. But I am sure that every parent who read the article — even those who disagreed with Molnar's antiwar stand — had to identify with his fears that his son might be killed.

For fear is one of the emotions common to the human condition. And commonality of feeling is what makes the personal essay work. While exactly the same things don't make all of us frightened, happy, sad, proud, perplexed or angry, we nonetheless share those emotions — not in the same proportions, perhaps, or with the same intensity. But whether we live in high-rise apartments or cabins in the forest, whether we are male or female, rich or not so prosperous, we can relate to these feelings in others.

As a result, some personal essays deal with pretty heavy stuff. Many of us have secret rooms in our lives that are too emotionally painful, embarrassing, frightening and/or depressing to let others enter. Because we're unable to talk about them, we often don't realize that other people have had similar experiences. So when writers are willing to shove open one or another of these doors to let readers look into their hidden rooms, they help those of us with the same problems/heartaches/fears to feel less alone. It's rather the same process that occurs in group therapy.

Most personal essays, however, aren't that intense. The majority of them deal with ordinary, nonthreatening slices of our everyday lives. Many are positively lighthearted with not a smidgen of soul-searching.

Take "All the Comforts of Home" by Freida Stewart in *Cooking Light*, for example. The blurb says, "When life deals me a bad day, I don't despair. I just go home and reach for the jar of peanut butter." The piece itself—640 words long—amplifies the blurb, telling about the writer's soothing relationship with peanut butter, from childhood to the present.

Another food-themed essay with a lighthearted touch, "Let *Them* Eat Cake," with the blurb "Because nothing tastes as good as being thin feels!" by Sharon Kay, was published by *Weight Watchers Magazine* in its "Food for Thought" department.

Although you'll find most personal essays with a food focus in food and wine magazines, they're popular in other kinds of publications as well. "Confessions of a Cranberry-Sauce Addict" appeared in *New Choices for the Best Years*; "A Question of Taste" in *Touring America*.

Nostalgic reminiscences are also best-sellers as far as essay themes are concerned. Strange as it may seem, recalling grandfather's stories, grandmother's kitchen, the lazy days of summer vacation, the corner store—although they've been recalled by a legion of writers before you—can result in article sales if your approach is fresh.

A variation of the nostalgic reminiscence flows from the common-to-most-of-us yearning to recapture some aspect of life as it was five or ten or fifty years ago. This kind of essay looks at a custom or condition that existed back in the "good old days." Personalization is provided by the author's point of view that says, "I wish it were still that way." This sort of wishing isn't confined to the over-fifty crowd by any means. Just talk to a twenty-three-year old for a while and you'll hear references to the good old days when you could buy baseball cards for a dime or a Barbie doll for less than five dollars.

The "how I coped with my problem" refrain is echoed again and again in personal essays. "Young Mother's Story" in *Redbook Magazine*, for example, tells how the authors came to grips with everything from long-repressed sexual abuse to raising a child with severe facial abnormalities.

Telling about an unusual experience and how it changed the writer's life/outlook is a serious essay theme that's closely related to that of problem-coping. The decision to donate your kidney to a twin sister's child, your thoughts while being held hostage, sorting out priorities while fleeing from the Khmer Rouge are the sorts of "life is earnest" topics these pieces are based on.

One word of caution here. Don't confuse the personal experience article with the personal essay. "My Day in the Duck Blind," a shot-by-shot report on hunting, would qualify as a personal experience. "My Day in the Duck Blind" spent philosophizing on the morality of hunting merely as sport would constitute a personal essay.

In sum, while the personal essay can evolve from a personal experience of some kind, it must focus on insights gained, lessons learned or opinions formed from that experience. The personal experience, by contrast, is simply the relating of an event.

Upon reading personal essays, you will find that most of them—even those in the serious vein—are woven around commonplace situations in which virtually all of us have found ourselves. Having a falling out with a friend, losing a loved one, facing a career challenge, dealing with financial decisions, accepting change, moving, and worrying about the world's problems are only a few of the hundreds of possible topics.

You'll find as many potential subjects on the lighter side. Buying a car, a home, a lawn mower. Choosing a pet, a name for the baby, a college for your teenager, a color scheme for your bedroom, or what to have for dinner. Having a party, a garage sale, a facelift. You can spend so much time making lists of possibilities that there won't be any left for writing.

Foibles, like the one my friend Shirley calls "straining on a gnat and swallowing an elephant," are popular essay topics with editors, too. The personal essay in which the writer can take some common shortcoming, spin personal experiences around it, laughing at herself all the way, is almost sure to be an editorial winner.

As far as I'm concerned, generating essay topics is easier than thinking of subjects for almost any other kind of article.

Just take a look at some of the personal essays that have appeared in the "First Person Parent" department of *Parents Magazine*. Although they're currently not written by freelancers, they are worth studying as idea generators.

"Grocery Store Blues" talks about going to the market when the children were due home from school in half an hour: the runaway shopping cart gouging the car in the parking lot; the crowded store; the misbehaving kid in the shopping cart, his mother soothing him by stroking his hair while she dodges his kicks; express-line crashers; the cereal box UPC that won't activate the "timesaving" scanner; the gum-cracking checker who pulls out a paper towel and starts cleaning the scanner. We've all been there. So has writer Elizabeth Berg, who was able to craft humor out of annoyance.

Another of Berg's essays in *Parents* explored "My Very Different Daughters" with the blurb "One is shy like me; the other is Miss Congeniality 2003." Not an especially earthshaking idea, granted, but a very effective one when treated cleverly.

Any of us can recreate our daily routines and come up with dozens of everyday themes. Using a gallon of gasoline so we can get to the nearest recycling center to turn in eighty-nine cents' worth of aluminum cans. Paying our kids a quarter a mile, a dime a lap, five cents for each time around the track when we would rather their energies be directed at mowing the lawn. Packing school lunches that always get traded for less nutritious food. The list can go on and on if you really think about it.

As mentioned earlier in the chapter, producing the personal essay requires "think" time in greater quantities than it does time to research and to write. And although thinking has been called the hardest thing in the world to do, it's an occupation that can be undertaken without benefit of a specific milieu, special equipment or within a prescribed structure. In fact, once you get an idea for a personal essay, snippets of thought relating to it will probably sneak into your consciousness when you least expect them to.

There are a couple of tricks I've discovered that help me get the most out of my thinking time. One is that notepad I keep in my purse. Whenever a specific portion of an article needs thinking about, I write it on the pad: "Come up with an anecdote about procrastinating" or "Think of another point illustrating honesty." Then, waiting in the drive-up line at the bank, I check my notes to see what I ought to be thinking about.

The other is to assign myself a writing problem before I start in on some mindless task like peeling potatoes or scouring the sink. While briefly focusing on a writing challenge often won't totally resolve it, the cumulative results of a number of short thinking sessions will.

PERSONALIZING YOUR ESSAY TO THE EDITOR'S PREFERENCE

Whether the personal essay makes us laugh or cry, whether it's about a life-and-death topic or an everyday aspect, it must be written in the style and format to which its intended readers are accustomed. Unlike most other article types, certain personal essays might fit into a number of different publications, but many of them must be precisely tailored to their intended publications in order to sell.

Take the monthly personal essays in *Glamour*, for instance. Information in *Writer's Market* under the magazine's listing says,

"Our His/Hers column features generally stylish essays on relationships or comments on current mores by male and female writers in alternate months." It would take a great deal of perception and a lot of luck, however, for a writer to put together a salable column for this feature on the basis of that information alone.

By reading personal essays previously published in *Glamour*, you'll find that the subject matter is really quite traditional (facing adversity, finding out about a family secret, meeting someone by chance who is connected to one's past, savoring the contents of Mother's dresser drawers). In the half-dozen pieces I read, nothing had to do with mores (the customs of a society), except that it was obvious when a significant other was mentioned that it was a live-in rather than a spouse.

By contrast, the personal essays in *Cosmopolitan*'s "his point of view" have a definite sexual focus. "Why Boys Like Bad Girls," "A (Wanna-Be) Rake's Progress" and "What Makes a Man Ache With Lust?" are typical. Upon reading the essays, however, you realize that the titles are more titillating than the prose that follows. "Bad girls" turn out to be girlfriends who ride roughshod over a man's ego; the wanna-be rake is a nice guy who thinks women go for men who, in the 1920s, would have been called cads; and the "lust" piece explores differences between infatuation-motivated and physical-urge sex.

Cosmo has a second personal essay department called "on my mind." Essay titles have included "The 'Accidental' Pregnancy: How Not to Capture a Man" and "Have You Caught the Baby Bug Yet?" Although *Glamour* and *Cosmo* are both women's magazines, a half hour's study will show you that their essays are definitely not interchangeable.

Other examples of tailoring the essay to fit its intended publication can be found on the back pages of *Women's Sports & Fitness*. In a department called "My Sport," each month's essay (they're usually 500 to 550 words in length) is written by a woman about her favorite way of exercising, be it scuba diving, mountain climbing, Tae Kwon Do or ice fishing.

Although the authors describe what it's physically like to swim on the ocean floor or survey their surroundings from the top of the world, the essays' purpose is more complex than merely describing the sport. These pieces allow readers to get inside the heads of the participants, to vicariously experience the other-than-physical benefits the sports provide. There's a lot of thought put to the body/mind connection in these pieces, and it's a necessary element of their sales success.

Passages like "My concentration is total; the worries of the day dissolve, meaningless. Early on, I concentrate on the art's sheer physicality—I feel strong and supple as I spar" and "Scuba diving has helped me surpass the limitations I had slowly been creating for myself. As middle age crept up, I slipped into a role of complacency. Facing new experiences brought feelings of fear rather than of challenge. But scuba diving has helped reverse that" give these pieces their personal essay quality.

The personal essays in *Victoria* have to relate in some way to furniture or other accoutrements and/or activities of the Victorian era. In each essay, no matter what the subject, there's an underlying theme of the writer's delight with things Victorian.

Class and family reunions, buying a house, going to the dentist—any common experience that involves feelings qualifies as a personal essay subject if you find a compatible market for it. And don't worry about an idea being unsalable just because it has already been written about. If your angle is a fresh one, almost any subject can take on new life. Take wedding anniversaries, for instance. Anyone who has read a number of personal essays is sure to have read anniversary pieces. But most likely not from the angle used by Hugh O'Neill in "The Day I Got Married," which appeared in *McCall's*.

It was a magical time. But why must I mark it each year?

In general, I'm a sucker for observance—holidays, rituals, commemoration. The big days get done up brown. Even modest anniversaries—including October 2, the day of Bucky Dent's epochal Red Sox-killing home run—get a private benediction from yours truly.

I am not only a connoisseur of remembrance, I am also inclined to the schmaltz of married life.

So when my sister mentioned the advent of my tenth wedding anniversary, I was surprised to find myself unmoved. Somehow a milestone that was supposed to be of some moment left me, a fool for ain't-we-grand, totally cold.

It made no sense. The day I got married was the best day of my life.

There was a chilly false spring in the Philadelphia air. Inside Jody's ancestral home, the flowers were not displayed but somehow in bloom, as though they had sprung up in our honor for that day. I remember perfume, party dresses and pearls, blue suits and snappy ties. I remember overcoats piled, cuddled on the bed upstairs. And I remember my brother. Part soldier, part sprite, the very model of ebullient formality, he seemed somehow to preside over the buoyance. I remember being nervous, not, God knows, about the wedding, but that Jody could escape down the trellis. I remember feeling the air in my lungs.

So how can I explain my cool about the return of that beloved date? It is—I'm happy to report—the tradition that's bankrupt, not this husband.

The problem with wedding anniversaries is not the idea but the formal manner in which they're observed. The engraved commemorative clichés have taken the sap out of the occasion.

Anniversaries count cadence to a waltz, take the improv out of the jazz. They are for finished things, a boast, a piety no match made in heaven can endure. I ask you: Would Michelangelo have arranged a sherry party in honor of getting halfway across the ceiling? No. There is a work in progress here. There are hopes to have, plans to change, hands to hold, jokes to get, apologies to make, affections for which to be grateful, maybe even children to tend. There is someone with whom to be in love.

Anniversaries feel false to me, like faint praise for an extravagant blessing. Raising a glass in a toast, I'm reminded of the guy who arrives on the rim of the Grand Canyon and says something about its beauty. He's not wrong, he's just a little noisy. Churches and marriages in full bloom make modest souls quiet.

I remember a bride wearing a blue dress and a big smile. She was young and light eyed, fully equipped with those lips and confidence in what was to come. I remember making promises about sickness and health. I was a knight. I wouldn't fail her; I'd be steadfast and full of fire. I was a knave as well; I couldn't possibly hold up my end of this deal.

I remember champagne, a piano full of music. I remember suit jackets tossed over the backs of chairs, neckties loosened in celebration. I remember a room made of hope. I remember the size and weight, the texture and promise of Jody in my arms. But mostly, looking back on that day, I remember starting to dance.

Our eleventh anniversary is now at hand, and I find myself still an apostle of occasions, and still curmudgeonly about this particular celebration, reluctant to make those vows anew. I meant them the first time. 'Nuff said. Like the tightrope walker, I'm disinclined to turn around or look too far ahead. I like it up here. I'm going to take this one step at a time.

I'm sure you'll agree that O'Neill's angle was all-important in selling his piece. The subject is a broad one; most people are, have been or anticipate being married. But his angle is not the usual one. However, it's one that strikes a responsive cord, I'll bet, with lots of readers.

O'Neill's style and development of his theme were persuasive selling points, too. His personality begins showing through in the lead and reader identification starts with those first paragraphs.

The technique of interspersing descriptions of the wedding day with his philosophy that the anniversary tradition is bankrupt along with accompanying rationale develops the theme gracefully. Without having to make obvious points, the writer is able to get his message across with a light touch.

Note the just-right adjectives and the enhancement of detail with an economy of words, always keeping in mind that the topic started off as a mundane one—the wedding anniversary. Like the subjects of all good personal essays, it was made special by the writer's skill.

Even though the number of potential personal essay topics is as great as your ingenuity, the one you choose must be given the personal approach. Consider the following lead sentences:

> My father used to follow me from room to room, turning off lights.

> When I was growing up, I knew from books and magazines what Thanksgiving should be like.

> Last time I was in the grocery store, I saw some frosting that could be put on cakes before they cooled.

To augment this personalization, almost every essay includes anecdotes or vignettes that allow the reader little peeks into the author's life, past or present. And although memories from the past are often an integral part of these pieces, don't confuse them with nostalgia. Nostalgia, as you know, looks yearningly at the past with rose-colored glasses. Personal essay remembrances are not necessarily pleasant.

THE EXPANDING ESSAY MARKET

We've talked at length about generating ideas and tailoring them to editors' specifications. But your options will be limited if you're aware of only a handful of publications.

Although the listings in *Writer's Market* are a good source of information, don't stop there. Since the trend toward personal essays is a strong one, each month a number of established magazines are altering their formats (if they haven't yet done so) to include them. And new publications make their newsstand debuts each month, offering additional market potential.

Spending a couple of lunch hours at the library and/or checking over the contents at the newsstand will pay big marketing dividends. You soon find that while most women's and religious magazines already have pages devoted to personal essays, a growing number of specialty magazines are using them as well.

You will even find personal essays in regional magazines. Some of them, like those in *Mpls.-St. Paul*, don't always have an area tie-in ("Teens and Money: Soon Parted" and "Thanksgiving for Two," were two articles printed in its "A Thousand Words" department. When you see this kind of essay, it's a good idea to find out whether being a local writer is a requisite for essay publication.

You'll also want to keep your eye out for closed circulation magazines (those that go to insurance company policyholders, automobile club or fraternal organization members, for example) and newspaper Sunday magazines. Short of shoplifting, glom onto every magazine you can and you're sure to come up with years' worth of personal essay prospects.

PERSONALITY ANALYSIS

Whereas it is important to query before writing nonfiction articles, most editors refuse to commit themselves on a personal essay until they've seen the whole piece of work. That means it will require your best shot to read the editor's mind. The best way to do that is by gathering together previously published essays from the magazine and analyzing their components.

Although these article ingredients vary with the publication, they remain basically:

1. Article length
2. Kind of lead
3. Amount of descriptive stage setting
4. Number of subpoints augmenting article's main thrust
5. Number of anecdotes
6. Amount of writer involvement
7. Point of view/tone
8. Breadth of focus
9. Type of ending

The names of the departments that personal essays appear in are often informative. "First Person Parent" subjects must have relevance to an extremely large segment of readers. Most of the people who read *Parents Magazine* have children. Most of them have experienced the same general situations written about. True, parents of an only child might not relate to the previously mentioned article about the two daughters, but most parents of two or more children, be they boys or girls, would.

Titles tell you a lot, too, for they go a long way in establishing the tone of a piece. You can be pretty sure that "Grandpa's Pond Mirrored Magical Moments" will be a nostalgic, serene piece. And chances are you won't get a lot of laughs from "Who Pays the Price for Drug-Related Crime?"

The best way to learn how to craft your personal essays is by reading those you find in top-paying publications. But be aware that you must study recent issues to be sure you will know what the editors are looking for. For example, in 1983, *Woman's Day* inaugurated a personal essay department called "Reflections." It appeared on the back page of each issue of the magazine. The subjects covered ranged from "The Secret to a Forever Marriage" to "On Finding the Perfect Christmas Gift." Then in the September 3, 1991, issue a department called "Back Talk" appeared on the magazine's last page. A change in tone came along with the new name. Pieces—as well as their titles—are less gentle and deal more with contemporary issues.

WRITE ON

When the scraps of paper with informational notes on them begin to pile up in your personal essay folder, it's time to start writing. Another indicator for me that writing time is at hand is that I develop a condition I refer to as "mind-spill": I've thought so much about an idea that the thoughts must go on paper to keep them in order—there's just too much material taking up conscious brain space.

The fact that personal essays are almost 1,000 words or less requires tight writing without losing the intimacy required for reader identification. Personal essay writers who, at the outset, don't narrow their focus sufficiently will find themselves in deep cutting trouble.

So keep in mind that personal essays almost always are based on a single premise: kids fight; it's hard to move to a new town; fashion fads are funny. But remember, too, that most premises are themes on which there can be all kinds of variations. To succeed, you must choose your particular variation and not be tempted to add others.

Another pitfall awaits the writer who prematurely chooses a subject that has affected him or her psychologically and fails to distinguish between writing for catharsis and writing a publishable essay. Cathartic writing is done during the process of dealing with a problem. The personal essay should be attempted only after the problem has been worked through.

A third difficulty arises when writers put too much of themselves into their articles. I-I-I pieces not only look awkward in print, they stand in the way of reader empathy. By judicious use of first person singular, you'll write much stronger pieces.

THE 30-MINUTE WRITER'S PLAN OF ACTION

1. Survey the markets to find out what magazines buy personal essays. Read essays in a variety of publications to determine whether you would like (or feel you would be competent) to write them.

2. Gather together several recent essays from your targeted publications, either by tearing the sheets from magazines or photocopying them. Put them in file folders with an identifying label.

3. Generate ideas for each publication by thinking of parallel topics. The editor who bought my "Farewell to Sunday Best" also bought "Waste Not, Want Not" from another writer. "A Stitch in Time," "Don't Cry Over Spilt Milk" and "A Penny Saved Is a Penny Earned" are obvious examples of themes that parallel the first two. There are also dozens of not-so-obvious ones.

4. Inventory your feelings and emotions. Think of experi-

ences that have given you insight into the human condition. Would any of those experiences be in keeping with your targeted editor's previous purchases? If you get stuck, lubricate your idea-generating mechanism by making lists of experiences common to large portions of any publication's readership: dieting, shaving, exercising, having regrets, losing sleep, paying bills, going to the dentist, getting married, raising children, buying shoes, going to movies, playing games, mailing packages, taking showers, eating dinner, cleaning closets, attending baseball games, being embarrassed, finding pennies. Once you have begun making lists, you'll find it's hard to turn the idea machine off.

5. Analyze the examples in your file to learn how they're put together and what components, such as adjectives, you will need to write your piece. Pay attention to the openings. Are they descriptive, anecdotal or narrative? What is the average length? In the body of the piece, how many points are made to reinforce the theme? How are they made—with anecdotes, quotes, descriptions of places or events? Does the ending take you by surprise? Does it summarize the article's premise or give it a twist? Let the results of your analysis be your guide.

6. Whenever you think of them—and your subconscious will be working on your article even when you're consciously working at something else—write down thoughts that have to do with your piece. Take some of your spare segments of time to purposely plumb your memory for anecdotes that might be used to illustrate the point/points you plan to make.

7. Make minioutlines of one or two of the publication's previously published essays, with the approximate number of words opposite each entry. The results could look something like this:

A. Anecdotal lead followed by summary sentence—250 words

B. Second anecdote illustrating premise—200 words

C. Two paragraphs of narrative regarding author's reaction to above—350 words

D. Closing anecdote with concluding summary statement—200 words

8. Start writing!

CHAPTER XI

Critic's Choice

Ranting and raving for pay is a skill that the wise 30-Minute Writer should consider acquiring. For writing reviews is the best way I know of combining business with pleasure.

People with time and money on their hands can buy all the books and tapes, attend all the theatre performances and ballets they like, never regretting the hours or dollars spent.

By the same token, the 30-Minute Writer — who's pressed for time and usually could use more money — can read those same books and attend those same plays for free by becoming a critic. And there are additional rewards. Although the books and records are the same you could buy at the store, I've found the complimentary performance seats are almost always better than any I could pay for at the box office. That's because the best seats in the house are either sold in advance to subscribers or kept available for people the sponsor wants to impress — the critics.

The late Clifton Fadiman once said, "True literary criticism is a venerable art. You can number the top-notchers on your fingers and toes." What Fadiman didn't say was that no top-notch reviewer is born a master of the venerable art. The first-rate critics rose to the top by taking advantage of their opportunities and serving a period of apprenticeship.

Reviewing is not for everyone. It is a demanding pursuit and one that leaves the reviewer open to a lot of slings and arrows.

Everyone loves to critique the critic. Payment for reviews is generally less than for articles of equal length, but there's a certain prestige to having your byline on reviews.

Of course, to become a successful reviewer, you have to know what you're talking about. To do a good job, your knowledge has to be more than superficial. In fact, you must know a great deal more about your subject than the general public. You have to either already be an expert on whatever you're reviewing or must truly love (and study) your chosen area so that you acquire the necessary expertise.

Rock reviewers who have studied guitar, opera reviewers who have taken voice lessons, and drama critics with theater backgrounds do a more competent job than they could without those experiences. People with a longtime interest in dance, books or artistic disciplines will find reviewing a gratifying blend of business and pleasure.

If you can't tell a jeté from a pas de deux, you had better learn or let someone else cover the ballet. Likewise, you had better have a thorough understanding of opera before you attempt to critique *Faust*.

Reviews aren't limited to classical forms. As you do your market research, you will find that there's a demand for commentary on contemporary music recordings, showroom and cabaret acts, movies, and television shows in addition to art exhibits, books, theater, musical comedy and other stage performances. But contemporary forms require no less background knowledge and homework than classical.

As a reviewer, you have an enormous responsibility. An unfavorable newspaper review of a fledgling string quartet may mean that its first concert will be the last. Big-city critics can make the difference between standing room only and an empty house. Careers often hang in the balance. The reviewer, like it or not, must at times play God.

That responsibility extends beyond the footlights to each potential member of the audience. After all, it's fifty dollars the reviewer is asking him to spend to see the revival of *42nd Street*, or is telling him to save instead of going to *The Magic Flute*.

The potential audience member looks to the critic's good judgment in deciding how to spend that hard-earned money, and that trust must never be taken lightly.

Breaking into review writing is easiest at the local level. Approach newspaper editors with copies of reviews you have written along with information on your credits and background: a college major in fine arts, theater experience and the like.

To find out which editors to contact, look at the newspaper's masthead or telephone their offices to ask for the name of the person in charge of reviews.

If you've never had work published, write two or three sample reviews to show the editor. Many newspapers have a policy of accepting no freebies, although this policy is often ignored in the case of review copies of books. If this is the case, the cost of your tickets or material to be reviewed will be paid by the newspaper.

There are still, however, a good many publications whose management believes that it is possible to maintain integrity even though tickets, books, and so on are supplied gratis. If this is the case, once you have established a working relationship, ask for a supply of the publication's stationery on which you can write future requests for performance tickets, records and review copies from publishers. Keep in mind that whatever items you receive should be used for their intended purpose and never sold or given as gifts.

Since most magazine reviews are written on assignment, send copies of your published newspaper reviews along with your qualifications to the editors you have in mind. If they like your presentation, the editors will either ask you to review specified works or suggest that you provide them with information on possible review subjects.

Surveying the magazine market will reveal a vast number of review possibilities, from *Opera News* to *Outside*. It's easy to analyze what the editors of these specialty magazines are looking for, since they use only commentaries on works directly related to their areas of specialization. Not surprisingly, you'll find reviews of books by or about people of Scandinavian descent in *Scandinavian Review*, records and performances featuring contemporary pop music for *Rolling Stone*.

Not only will you find that there's a vast market for reviews of the arts, there's an equally big one for product reviews. Since Chopin is a far cry from cat food, we'll discuss the two categories separately, beginning with the arts.

BOOK REVIEW BASICS

Although reviews of movies and live performances often outnumber those of books in newspapers, the majority of reviews in magazines focus on the printed page. And they're especially suited to 30-Minute Writers who read every chance they get, whether they can spare the time or not.

Like reviews of all art forms, book reviews can be classified as 1.) objective and 2.) subjective. An objective review emphasizes the work—its aim and scope—and the special qualifications of the writer to write the book. Whereas the objective review was fairly common a decade or two ago, they're not as popular as they were. The following review, "Getting Stronger," by exercise physiologist Tod Iseminger, appeared in *Cooking Light* and is as close to being objective as most book reviews in contemporary magazines:

Shelter Publications, Inc.
P.O. Box 279
Bolinas, California 94924
$12.95 plus $2 shipping (paperback)

Getting Stronger, a comprehensive, step-by-step reference, specializes in strength training. Regardless of your age, sex, or ability, this book offers the accurate information vital for success in any type of weight-training program.

Subjects include general conditioning, bodybuilding, strength training for sports, and specialty exercises for fine-tuning individual muscle groups. Also included are sports and recreational training programs to get you or keep you in shape for a number of activities ranging from golf and volleyball to tennis and downhill skiing. Each section provides a detailed set of drawings and an in-depth description of how to perform the exercises safely. These descriptions are presented in a systematic, well-planned format so people can easily use the ideas in their own fitness programs.

In addition to excellent content on strength training, the book also covers related subjects, such as nutrition, injury prevention and treatment, and muscle physiology.

This thorough book is a first-rate resource for the competitive athlete (or any personal fitness library).

Notice that while the author makes statements such as "this book offers the accurate information vital for success," he refrains from analyzing about the author's motivation, intent, choice of words and the like, thus maintaining the review's objectivity. He merely tells what the book is about and evaluates its usefulness in an objective manner.

The more subjective reviews require additional thinking time, since the emphasis is on the reviewer's reaction to and evaluation of the book. This thoughtful review by Edward Allen appeared in the *New York Times Book Review*. Its subject is a book called *In the Land of Men* by Antonya Nelson (William Morrow & Company, $19, 239 pp).

Almost all the stories in Antonya Nelson's second short-story collection, *In the Land of Men*, take place in a sort of aftermath. We come upon her characters when their lives have already been fractured, displaced, uprooted. The events that have set these people adrift exist in retrospect; what Ms. Nelson shows us are not crises but rather lives set in a disconnected post-crisis landscape.

Geographic displacement and family fracture hang above these stories with the glum solidity of an overcast day in Ms. Nelson's vividly rendered Midwest. Those two themes come together most clearly in "Here on Earth," in which a teen-age girl accompanies her divorced mother on a business trip from their home in Phoenix to their former home in Chicago, a city whose sights are all dimmed by the father's obtrusive absence.

In "Adobe," the best story in the book, the narrator, a 40-year-old woman, has taken refuge in the Southwest after losing both her husbands not to death but to younger women. As she lets herself be drawn into an affair with a young, homeless Chicano laborer who has been helping to build her new house, she says, "That he is wrong for me in a hundred ways, and that I am to be deeply hurt, I dismiss by an act of will." This refusal (on the part of both the author and the character) to be either self-deluding or cynical is what makes the story, and the whole collection, so powerful. At the heart of all these stories is the sense of emotional life played for keeps.

I hope the misleadingly narrow title does not keep readers away. If people pass up "In the Land of Men" under the impression that it is going to be some sort of polemic, that will be a shame. It is as unpolemical as it can be, and Ms. Nelson's generosity is in no way gender-specific. The only thing I can find wrong is that a few of the stories, like "Bare Knees" and "Inertia," fall short of involving the reader emotionally, and that the author has a habit of ending stories, including some of the better ones, with unconvincing expository codas. But even in the lesser efforts, the detail and sense of place are so strong that they earn their keep alongside the truly fine pieces.

One reason the title is a problem is that only in the excellent but untypical title story is male stupidity the controlling factor. The most remarkable thing about this story—a rape victim's brothers kidnap the man they think is the perpetrator and leave it to her to decide whether he shall live or die—is Ms. Nelson's refusal, even when faced with the most emotionally loaded of subjects, to be lured into melodrama. The narrator recalls that in the aftermath of her attack "I prepared myself for nightmares, as instructed, but never had any directly related to that night."

Elsewhere, men and women are pretty much equally at liberty to make their own mistakes. Some stories, like "The Control Group," take place more in a land of women than a land of men.

In that strange story, a boy effectively orphaned by his mother's criminality pursues a completely serious courtship of his fourth-grade teacher. This story is pulled off with not a flicker of cuteness.

Something covert is usually peeking up through the surface of these narratives. For Nicole in "Fort Despair," the image of her younger brother's penis (he once exposed himself in the back seat of the family car) keeps encroaching upon her teen-age consciousness as insidiously as do the warning signs of her parents' imminent breakup. On "The Happy Day" of an affluent wedding, the photographer's slightly flaky assistant, Beth, is able to see in the play of children a Lilliputian re-enactment of the compromised and degenerate relationships that are being institutionalized by that day's ceremony.

Geographically, *In the Land of Men* is bifocal, with almost all stories taking place either in the Midwest or in the Southwest, and sometimes shuttling between the two. The Midwest, particularly Chicago, seems the place of stability, of origin, of coherence. The Southwest, rendered in arid clairty in stories like "Adobe" and "The Fact of Air," seems that unshaped and traditionless sandbox of those who have been uprooted, usually by broken marriages, from the moister loam of the heartland.

These are wonderful stories. In the most serious sense of the word, they are *kind* stories. What holds them together as an emotional unit is Antonya Nelson's unsentimental generosity toward her characters, her perfectionism about detail, and most of all her understanding that unhappiness is not tragic — it's just a fact of life. That sense of unhappiness as a norm, as a workaday precinct in which we sharpen our pencils and get on with the day's business, is curiously uplifting.

Allen's critique exemplifies an important characteristic you'll find in all good subjective reviews: he shows the reader instead of just stating opinions. His points are illustrated with examples. His adjectives are chosen carefully to convey the feeling Allen wants them to. The review is a balanced one, pointing out both the strengths and perceived shortcomings of the book, while synopsizing its primary premises.

Experts advise that, to maintain your integrity, you should never read the jacket copy, publishers' handouts or other reviews of the book before you write your own. Always read the entire work, they say, and *never ever* review a book you haven't understood.

Don't worry about having to spend hours reading a book you can't understand. When an editor assigns you a book to review, you'll know after a few pages whether it's one you're capable of writing about. If it is beyond you, let the editor know right away that the subject matter isn't within your area of expertise.

When writing reviews of fictional works, indicate the kind of book (gothic, mystery, horror) and give the time of the story and the setting. Supply information about the characters, but under no circumstances reveal a surprise ending. You may hint that it is unexpected, but say no more.

Questions you should answer in the nonfiction review concern the author's premise, the intrinsic significance of the work, unique qualities (if any) and the book's accuracy.

In subjectively reviewing both fiction and nonfiction, compare the book with others in the genre or on the same subject as well as previous books by the same author. Beware of the halo effect. Just because the writer's last book was a mainstream masterpiece doesn't necessarily mean that every book he writes will measure up. Point out strengths and weaknesses of style and content, giving reasons for both positive and negative criticisms.

Whatever type of review the publication calls for, don't neglect to mention the title of the book, its author's name, the price and number of pages. When applicable, include translators' names and all the editors of anthologies. Be sure that all of this information is accurate.

CRITIQUING CDS, VIDEOS, TAPES AND OTHER RECORDINGS

Reviews of recorded music are often shorter than those of books and are almost always subjective. The typical format contains a description and evaluation of the music, including instrumentation and arrangements, musicianship, and sometimes comparison with previous recordings by the same artist(s) or those of other performers. The tone of music reviews complements the kind of music written about — classical reviews are almost always more formal than those of contemporary musical styles. The lead from this review by Kevin Powell in *Rolling Stone* of "Juice" reflects the tunes in the album:

> In hip-hop culture, B-Boys use the term *juice* to describe their street-level power and prowess. The all-star soundtrack from Ernest Dickerson's *Juice* spills over with this type of self-assuredness. Produced by Hank Schocklee of Public Enemy fame, the album is agit-rap and R&B at its grittiest levels: Shocklee's trademark shrill noises are omnipresent, as are hundreds of sonic blasts meshed with riveting vocals and live instruments. The effect is hypnotic; the album's cross-fertilization of beats and grooves leaves one squarely in the young lions' den of urban America."

Contrast that lead with the one that followed it in the magazine, appearing in a review by Daisann McLane of Linda Ronstadt's "Mas Canciones" and Ana Gabriel's "Mi Mexico":

> Linda Ronstadt probably has the most beautiful and technically accomplished voice ever to grace a Mexican *ranchera*. On *Mas Canciones*, her second collection of Mexican songs, Ronstadt's pristine, bell-shaped chest tones, clear falsetto and controlled sobs compete with the crystalline strings and trumpets of the Mariachi Vargas de Tecalitlan orchestra for sheer prettiness. The trouble is that the Mexican *ranchera* is not quaint traditional music. A theater of human emotions, written in vernacular poetry of pain, pride and sexual braggadocio, *ranchera* is dramatic, at times hyperbolic, never merely pretty. Mexico's beloved pantheon of great female stars, from Lucha Reyes to Amalia Mendoza and Lola Beltran (who seems to be Ronstadt's model in this genre), cannot match Ronstadt's tonal purity, and they sometimes hit notes flat or sharp. But their gritty

cries and explosive crescendos raise goose bumps. Ronstadt does not, and in ranchera, goose bumps rule.

In the excerpts above, it's obvious that the authors know what they're writing about. Powell's choice of hip words enhances his description of the musical style he's reviewing. McLane's knowledge of female Mexican vocalists, their techniques and recordings (as well as the ranchera genre) gives a depth to her review that's the mark of a professional.

It's imperative that the reviewer be familiar with the artist's other works and the genre in general if she is to write a quality review. Although you don't have to possess a great deal of musical ability to be a record critic, you must be well versed in the musical idiom you're writing about.

When the publication doesn't furnish them, the best way to get tapes, CDs and videos is by contacting the companies that produce them or agents representing their artists. Unless you include copies of published reviews you have written, however, you probably won't be too successful in obtaining work by well-known musicians. There are, however, multitudes of people who have recorded and are dying to have their music reviewed.

After any agent or recording company is convinced on the basis of reviews you have submitted to them that you are worth investing a certain amount of inventory in, you will probably be deluged with material. The easiest way to get the names and addresses of record companies is by going to the nearest record store and asking to see their "phonolog," which contains information on recordings currently available.

Another way to do the job is by making friends with a disc jockey. DJs are bombarded with complimentary recordings and should be agreeable to letting you borrow albums for a day or two at a time. Although many libraries lend tapes as well as books, by the time they acquire them, it's almost always well after their release dates.

SNEAK PREVIEWING

Also highly subjective, the most popular form of movie review emphasizes plot, performances by the various actors, and overall production. A critique of cinematography and special effects, as well as background information on where the film was shot and any special problems that had to be overcome, should be included when relevant. You can get this info from the releasing studio's public relations department, but be aware that a lot of hype may be mixed in with what actually happened.

The movie reviews in the *San Francisco Chronicle*'s "Datebook" are especially well crafted and complete. Their writers interview actors and/or directors for insights into the films, giving added depth to the reviews. The following excerpts from a review of "The Inner Circle" by Kristine McKenna, a Los Angeles-based writer who covers the arts, will show you how packed with information a top-rate review is, and will provide an example of the kind of "inside information" editors go for:

> Josef Stalin died 38 years ago, but his shadow lingers over the people he forced into submission for 31 years. Establishing a link between Stalin, the history of oppression in the former Soviet Union and the problems the people there face as they stumble toward freedom is the focus of "The Inner Circle," a new film by Russian director Andrei Konchalovsky.
>
> Based on an idea that came to Konchalovsky more than twenty years ago when he met a film projectionist who had worked for Stalin, the film is a loosely fictionalized version of the life of Alexander Ganshin, a simple working-class man (played in the film by Tom Hulce) who screened movies for Stalin from 1935 until his death in 1953 and thus became a member of Stalin's envied and feared inner circle. . . .
>
> One of the points the film attempts to make is that monsters such as Stalin don't spring up from external sources and attack a people from the outside; rather, they arise from deep within the hearts of those they dominate and are a dark manifestation of a culture's collective subconscious. . . .

"I made Stalin charismatic because I wanted him to be seen as he was through the eyes of his admirers, and because I believe that ultimate evil often dresses in the most attractive dress," says Konchalovsky.

"I love this character Ivan and want the viewer to understand how desperate he was and how terrible it will be for him when he starts to understand the reality of his life. When he starts to wake up, it's as painful as if he'd had frozen limbs that were beginning to defrost. His soul was frozen and when it begins to thaw he must struggle with the question of why he lives in a society that makes people do such bad things."

Taking notes in a darkened theater presents problems. A technique I've found useful is to write each thought, sentence or other piece of information on a separate sheet of a small note pad, putting each of them into your briefcase when you've finished. That way, you won't write one sentence on top of another.

If possible, transcribe the notes as soon as you get home and add other details while they're fresh in your mind. You'll usually not need to see the movie twice if you've taken effective notes. However, in the case of complex plots and foreign films, a second viewing makes your job easier.

As with any other kind of review, you'll need to match your tone with the subject matter. Writing about a knuckle-biting thriller, a slapstick comedy and a historical romance in the same voice won't make you a box-office hit with any editor.

Since most movie reviews are between 300 and 800 words long, you have to jump right into your subject with the lead, as McKenna did with her "Inner Circle" review.

When you're synopsizing the plot, you can organize your material in logical progression like McKenna did, tucking in information about production costs, the director's background and cinematic goals, stellar performances and other pertinent subjects along the way (you can often get production facts and figures from the company that made the film).

PERFECTING YOUR PERFORMANCE

You can reread books and listen to tapes over and over without it costing you money, but in most cases you'll only be given one ticket for each live performance. To write a quality review, therefore, you will need to prepare for the performance.

If possible, become familiar with the performance facility—concert hall, amphitheater, nightclub—in advance. Find out where acoustics are poor and where viewing is impaired so you can alert potential ticket buyers to the problem.

Learn whatever you can about the star performers' previous experience: where the prima ballerina got her training, under whom the conductor studied, and so forth. If you can, get background information on minor performers, too. One of them might steal the show and your advance planning will save you from scurrying around for info while battling a deadline.

Read the play, study the libretto, listen to recordings of the music before you go to a performance. Skimming the program notes during intermission won't be adequate, nor will it be fair to the performers or your readers.

Make a checklist of things you'll want to note during the actual performance and memorize it. If you're reviewing a play, opera, ballet or musical comedy, include on your list such items as lighting, sets and special effects, leaving room for evaluations of individual artists' performances as well.

When the production involves music, whether it is a symphony or a country-western concert, list such criteria as choice of material, pacing and quality of musicianship. Ask yourself whether the program is balanced: Do the various selections complement one another? Is their sequence pleasing?

One of the perennial questions that plague reviewers is whether it is fair to use the same standards of judgment for a little-theater production in, say, Fargo, North Dakota, as for a play on Broadway. Before you embark on a reviewing career, decide whether your standards will be absolute or relative.

PICTURES AT AN EXHIBITION

Before you visit an art exhibit you plan to review, you'll save time
and frustration if you make a list. A clipboard is handy, I've found,
for this sort of review viewing. If brochures listing the exhibited
works are available, arrange to obtain one for advance study. Here
are some of the questions you will want to ask yourself when
you're on the scene:

1. Is the quality consistent?
2. Which of the works are most outstanding?
3. Has the purpose of the exhibit been accomplished? For example, does it chronicle the artist's creative progression, provide a representational sampling of work in the genre, present a unifying theme?
4. Are any unusual media involved?
5. During what time period were the works completed?
6. Is the exhibit worth traveling an hour and/or paying money to see? Why? Why not?

Reviews of exhibits featuring painting, sculpture and other
forms of art are published more frequently in big city papers and
magazines because more big-name exhibits are presented in metropolitan areas. However, newspapers in smaller cities and towns
may not use reviews on local art shows simply because no one has
come forth to write them.

Qualifications required (a background in fine arts and/or self-
educated appreciation) take time to acquire, but if you already
have them, you'll find reviewing fits in with your thirty-minute
time frame.

While attending the exhibits should be pure pleasure even
while you're taking notes, writing reviews will take some effort.
You can minimize the job, however, by patterning your pieces
after those previously published. Tone mirrors the seriousness of
the works reviewed: a formal tone for classical art, a light touch
for work that is satirical or whimsical, and a tone that's somewhere
in between for styles such as primitive, contemporary and pop.

Comparisons with works by other artists and with earlier
works by the exhibiting artist are elements you'll find in most

reviews. Style, technique and the artist's inspiration are almost always mentioned, too.

PLAYING TO THE AUDIENCE

The cardinal rule for any kind of reviewing is to keep your readers in mind always. Almost all fall into three groups: people who use reviews as guides to their book, tape, movie, TV program or live entertainment choices; people who want to know what's going on in the arts; and those who, having read a book, listened to a CD, watched a TV show, or attended a movie, art exhibit or performance, want to know what others have to say about it. A good review usually appeals to all three groups, since it describes or synopsizes—or at least hits the high points of—the work, likens or contrasts it to other works/artists, and evaluates it.

Built into your role as reviewer are certain obligations to these readers. Although imaginative writing enhances a review, if you're too clever you will obscure the purpose of the piece. And even though you have an extensive background in the genre, don't be esoteric or highbrow. You may impress readers with your knowledge, but you won't be fulfilling your function as a reviewer.

Don't let personal feelings get in your way. You may disagree with the author's point of view, but that is not in itself sufficient reason to warrant condemnation of a work. Never let your prejudices color your conclusions. Don't quote out of context, misrepresent, or omit material because of a personal bias.

Striking and maintaining the delicate balance between honest subjectivity and that based on personal feelings can be difficult. While it's completely cricket to let personal opinion based on solid knowledge determine what you write, beware of personal foibles. For example, when shades of purple—a color you detest—predominate in an art exhibit you're supposed to review, you'll either have to rise above your personal distaste or let the reader know why you may be less than enthusiastic. A third option is to disqualify yourself from writing the review because of your prejudices.

The hallmark of a first-rate reviewer is credibility. You'll want readers to know that when they see your byline they can believe what they read, that you won't give them bad advice on spending their entertainment dollars. So don't exaggerate. Be precise and honest.

When a performance is top drawer, say so. But if the play is cliché-ridden, its plot hackneyed, and the actors all seem to have overdosed with Valium, tell it like it is, even if the female star is your sister-in-law. However, before you scathe, do become knowledgeable about the "fair comment" provisions of press law. You'll find that while you can call a work of art or a single performance unredeemable trash ("Clara Voyant was a theatrical disaster from the time the curtain rose on 'The Fortune Telling Bride,' forgetting her lines, trying to upstage her co-star and looking more like the Bride of Frankenstein than a newly married woman of twenty-five"), your comment that the artist is incapable of producing anything of value ("Clara Voyant is a terrible actress and dooms any play in which she appears to failure") can land you in court. Even sisters-in-law can sue.

To hone your critiquing skills, study the reviews in such publications as the *New York Times*, *Christian Science Monitor*, *Atlantic* and *The New Yorker*. You'll note that well-crafted reviews have verve and punch, often attained by the use of similes and carefully chosen adjectives. They also achieve good balance between description and evaluation of content and style. Their authors are specific, avoiding overused words like *brilliant, boring, pleasant, pretty, interesting* and *nice*.

You'll score editorial curtain calls if you are scrupulous about submitting reviews of the required length. If word limits aren't spelled out, count words in a half-dozen previously printed reviews in the publication and work within that range. Be sure the review arrives at the publication in good condition, on time and directed to the proper person. If for some reason you cannot handle an assignment, notify the editor at once.

Reviewing the arts is perhaps the least lucrative of the short forms if you calculate gain as the ratio between time spent and payment. But if you look at reviewing in terms of the enjoyment it offers, the contacts you will make, and the stimulation of being center stage in the cultural scene, it can be one of the most rewarding forms of professional writing.

PANNING AND PRAISING PRODUCTS

Maybe it was Ralph Nader who started it, but in the past thirty years or so, consumers have become increasingly conscious of the qualities of products they're planning to buy. They weigh this lawnmower against that, these ski bindings against those. And much of the information they use comes from product reviews, especially the reviews they read in specialized magazines.

While much of this type of information can be found in consumer report types of publications, that usually means a trip to the library. So the product critiques readers can find in the magazines they read are a real boon.

In order to qualify as a product reviewer, you have to be an expert on your subject—perhaps you bicycle from coast to coast every vacation, or you've raised horses for twenty years, or your hobby is horticulture.

If that's the case, you probably have a head start on review marketing because of the publications you read. Scuba diving 30-Minute Writers know, for example, that *Skin Diver* publishes extensive reviews of scuba equipment such as camcorders that can be used for underwater photography. Backpackers are already familiar with the reviews of gear in *Backpacker*.

But even the most avid enthusiasts may not usually read all the publications that focus on their favorite activity. By looking through *Writer's Market*, you can find out about other publications that use reviews of items you're qualified to write about.

When you're looking through *Writer's Market* want lists, however, don't confuse "new product" with "review" needs. The former, with titles like "Toyota to Debut New Full-Size Pickup" and "Le Creuset Adds New Styles to Cookware Line," are brief, noncritical articles that tell about products that have recently come on the market.

Computer magazines are perhaps the largest market for product reviews. But the top-notch reviewer, in addition to being highly computer literate, knows that while some publications use reviews that go from one end of the computer spectrum to the other, many magazines are very specific as to what they want. Woe be unto the hapless reviewer who submits critiques of Macintosh software to *Shareware Magazine* or of Tandy computers to *Atari Explorer*.

The tone of product reviews is usually fairly serious, the writing without frills. The job of the reviewer is to educate, not impress. Communication is the key. Here's a no-nonsense review on "Waveflo Seat Pads" by Rob Story in *Outside*:

> Wheelchair technology has finally come to the bicycle. A hydraulic cushioning system originally developed for wheelchair seats is now being used in a line of bike seat covers. The manufacturer says Waveflo covers are more efficient—and 75 percent lighter—than their gel counterparts.
>
> Waveflo covers are padded with plastic packets of a substance called Flolite Liquid. The slow-moving goo is pushed away from areas where you're exerting a lot of pressure to areas where you're not; it stops when your weight is more or less stable and evenly distributed over the saddle. That's the theory. In reality, you'll still feel your pressure points, just not as intensely. But some relief is really all you can hope for, and Waveflo covers don't disappoint.
>
> I expected the increased comfort. But there was another benefit I hadn't counted on: added stability, especially from the two models with more liquid. The Seventh Wave (for road riding; $29) and the Totally Tubular (for mountain biking; $32) kept me almost stationary on the bike. The Tidal Wave ($27), on the other hand, is intended for triathletes and other racers, and I found its padding somewhat Spartan.
>
> Two caveats: Don't use a Waveflo cover with a gel saddle—the extra squish feels like you're riding a waterbed. And take your Waveflo with you when you lock up; a thief found the splashy Lycra exterior of my Tidal Wave too much to ignore.
>
> From Triple Sport Inc., Box 321, Boulder, Colo. 80306; (303) 939-9936.

Product reviewers usually get to try out the items they're reviewing without having to pay for them. I know a photographer who always goes on shoots with the latest in photographic equipment; another acquaintance always seems to be driving a different new automobile. Not all of us get to review cameras and cars, of course. But someone's got to do it. Maybe you.

THE 30-MINUTE WRITER'S PLAN OF ACTION

1. Become familiar with both the markets for reviews and the kinds of reviews used by each of the publications you enjoy reading.

2. Decide which kinds of reviews you would be qualified to write.

3. Attend performances, listen to new tapes, go to art exhibits and write reviews about them, patterning them after publications you wish to write for.

4. Write up a short résumé including your writing credits/ experience and qualifications as a reviewer.

5. Phone the editor of your local newspaper and/or any local magazines that publish reviews. Ask for an appointment.

6. At the appointment, give the editor a short verbal pitch on your qualifications as a reviewer. If he or she is interested, a discussion of how the selection of review materials is to be made and rates of payment should follow. Whether or not the editor seems interested, leave copies of your reviews and mini-résumé.

7. Send copies of appropriate reviews and your résumé to regional and national publications you would like to write for, along with a short cover letter. If your reviews are well written, your credentials solid, and you contact enough editors (persistence is one of the major names of the writing game), you'll likely see your name in editorial lights.

CHAPTER XII

The Competitive Edge

Contesting is one of the most potentially exciting paths the 30-Minute Writer can choose to follow, since writing and creativity are the skills needed to create winning contest entries. And they're the skills that prompt most of us to become 30-Minute Writers in the first place.

Entering contests can be lucrative, too. Top prizes in the major recipe competitions are big. In the 1992 Pillsbury Bake-Off Cooking & Baking Contest, $136,000 in prizes was awarded, including the grand prize of $40,000, six $10,000 category prizes, and eighteen prizes of $2,000 each. The one hundred finalists were also given all-expenses-paid-trips for two to Disneyworld, with spending money.

The National Chicken Cook-Off for 1991 offered a $25,000 first prize; $5,000, second; $3,000, third; $2,000, fourth; and $1,000, fifth; and all-expenses-paid-trips to Little Rock for a finalist from each state and the District of Columbia.

Prizes in the more than seventy-five major contests held during 1991 ranged from a five-day vacation at La Costa Spa in California to lunch with Paul Newman. Many of the competitions rewarded top winners with cash; one top prize was a Chrysler LeBaron.

For me, the best aspect of contesting (rather than winning) is that I can pursue the prizes by using only odd scraps of time. Winning ideas develop gradually—sixty seconds here, sixty seconds there.

If you need a success story to convince you, consider this:

About eleven years ago, I was stirring up a chowder called "Oyster Stewpendous" in the home ec room of a middle school in Leonardtown, Maryland, convinced that I hadn't a chance of winning the annual Oyster Festival cook-off. After all, I'd only been entering contests for less than a year and had spent precious little time at it. A few hours later, after having received the grand prize and a silver platter commemorating the event, I was forever hooked on contest cooking.

Since then, I've won a lot of great prizes: a Mississippi River cruise, a $1,300 barbecue grill that does everything except tap dance, checks for varying amounts of money, and enough electric frypans to keep us in wedding gifts for the next decade.

Along the way, I've made lots of contesting friends. Some of them win with amazing regularity. One of them has been a three-time finalist in the Pillsbury Bake-Off, gone to Hawaii as a finalist in the Pineapple Cook-Off, taken top place in the National Beef Cook-Off, and won hundreds of cash and merchandise prizes. Another has won trips to cooking schools and enough money to buy a car, put a new roof on the house, and establish a sizable college fund for her children.

Most of the people who win big win often. There's nothing rigged about it. They have simply developed a knack for knowing what will please the judges.

This knack, I am convinced, is a natural for writers to acquire. No matter what we may think at times, it *is* easier for us to come up with ideas and titles and to put words together because we've had more practice doing it.

Writers have the benefit of other experiences, too. They've learned that the first idea to flit across the mind has probably popped into lots of other heads as well—the "simultaneous invention" phenomenon. They are able to refine their ideas, change them, make them truly original and therefore more likely to be winners.

Writers also have had more experience with evaluating their own work and know which efforts are their best and which are only so-so. Analyzing winning entries requires the same skills as analyzing articles or stories.

Putting together entries is especially geared to 30-Minute Writers because contesting mostly involves thinking time, time when you are doing routine tasks and can let your creative mind wander. The physical preparation of entries takes only minutes.

FINDING THE COMPETITION

To win contests you have to know where to find out about them. They're often advertised in newspapers and magazines (especially *McCall's*, *Good Housekeeping*, *Family Circle*, *Woman's Day* and other women's publications). Two very good recipe contest bulletins are currently being published. Subscription rates are under twenty dollars for one year's monthly issues. The bulletins are:

Blue Ribbon Cooks' Newsletter
P.O. Box 711, Dept. P
Alhambra, CA 91802

Cooking Contest Chronicle
P.O. Box 10792, Dept. P
Merrillville, IN 46411

Other bulletins are published, but the bulk of the information in most of them is about sweepstakes. Although there are techniques to entering sweepstakes, we'll concentrate on skill contests in this chapter, since they're the only kind that give the writer an edge.

The majority of today's skill contests involve the creation (and sometimes preparation) of recipes. Winners of some of the food contests are chosen solely on the basis of their recipes. Others are selected as finalists because of their recipes but must, along with the other finalists, prepare those recipes for judges.

Though there are fewer statement, jingle and naming contests, their prizes are equally worth winning. For example, *Good Housekeeping*'s "Experience of a Lifetime" required contestants to complete in 150 words or less a sentence that began "The special experience that brought my family closer together was . . ." First prize was a trip to London for a family of four plus two thousand dollars in spending money and another thousand for theater tickets. Ronald McDonald's Family Theater was a cosponsor of the contest.

At about the same time, Fantastik household products in conjunction with *Family Circle* sponsored a 200-word essay contest on the theme "Why my family is the New American Family." Top prize in that competition was five thousand dollars, cash.

Many magazines sponsor contests, most of them on an irregular basis. Some, however, have competitions in each issue. Occasionally, these competitions are listed in contest bulletins, but the only way you can find out about the majority of them is by looking through lots of magazines — perhaps while you are doing marketing research for other projects.

You'll find, for example, that in each issue *Better Homes and Gardens* chooses two "Cooks of the Month," who get $200 each for their recipes, two runners-up who each receive $100, and six honor roll winners who receive food processors. The recipe categories change every month and are announced about thirty days in advance of entry deadline dates.

Magazines like *Family Circle* and *Woman's Day* present contests, such as "How to Get George Bush to Eat Broccoli," on an occasional basis. The value of the prizes varies with each contest, but they usually consist of sizable cash awards.

Be on the lookout, too, for local contests. Business-sponsored contests are usually announced in newspapers, and newspapers themselves sometimes conduct competitions.

COOKING UP A WINNER

Many parallel skills are employed by writers and recipe creators. First of all, there's finding an angle. To have a chance in national competitions, recipes have to be innovative. They can be updated versions of old favorites or variations on popular themes, but the angle must be a fresh one. And each recipe, like every article, must have an appropriate title — often a clever one.

Second, writers and recipe creators must be aware of trends. Just as the successful writer knows that short nonfiction articles are the hottest sellers today, the recipe contester who's a consistent winner can name the year's trendy ingredients at the flip of a spatula.

Then, too, both writers and recipe contesters must be able to say what they mean, must have a sense of structure, must pay attention to details and accuracy. They must have the ability to write visually, whether in an article about winemaking in the Rhine Valley or in a recipe for Icelandic wine cake.

Most recipe contests are sponsored by food companies and by groups whose purpose is to advertise and encourage the use of a specific brand or a kind of food, such as veal, potatoes or pineapple. Many of the winning recipes are used in advertising (on the products' packages or labels, in booklets and magazine ads, and so on).

Highlighting the Featured Ingredient. In creating your recipes, the main point to remember is that the sponsor is putting on the contest to promote its product. Emphasis should be put on enhancement if the sponsor is promoting a generic food. If you enter a contest calling for recipes using fish, for instance, devise one that emphasizes the fish flavor. Perhaps your favorite recipe does disguise the fish taste and therefore appeals to your fish-resistant family, but that's not the recipe to send in.

Too Many Steps Spoil the Spoils. Simplify procedures as much as you can without sacrificing taste. Recipes that are complex rarely win prizes. Janet Hill of Sacramento, California, who is one of the most successful cooking contesters in the country, says, "After I've finished working on a recipe, I set it aside. Then later, I go over it to see if I can simplify it." Hill, whose prizes have included a trip to Italy and a $100,000 savings bond, also believes that it's important not to create recipes that have too many ingredients.

Choose ingredients that will not only taste good together, but will make the dish look attractive, too. Contester Shirley DeSantis of East Windsor, New Jersey, once told me about a delicious recipe she had originated but would never submit because it looked like "Pepto Bismol with lumps."

Be creative and original, but don't be too innovative. Take a good basic recipe and give it a new twist. When Marjorie Ohrnstein of Los Angeles finished high school, her father gave her the choice of a new car or a course at Cordon Bleu (she chose Cordon Bleu). Today Ohrnstein, who's a consistent recipe contest winner, gets inspiration from her collection of more than five thousand cookbooks. "I read a cookbook like you would a novel," she says. "Usually, I get the basic framework from cookbooks prior to 1950, then I update the recipe."

Aim for ease of preparation. Your recipe should be one that can be made by an average cook in a reasonable length of time. Use only ingredients that are easy to obtain and appropriate to the contest's theme. If the sponsor calls for budget dishes, don't enter one that calls for imported mushrooms or saffron.

Remember that the judges are looking for recipes that purchasers of the product will want to duplicate in their own kitchens, so combinations of ingredients can't be too exotic. And by all means, try the recipe out in your kitchen before you submit it. The way to a judge's heart is not through heartburn.

If the finished product is a success, you need try the recipe only once. There's no need to seek reactions from people other than your family (friends, out of politeness, are usually unreliable) unless your food preferences are not those of most people.

Fitting Recipes to Recipients. Find recipes the sponsor has liked in the past, such as those printed on the product's package. They will give not only an idea of the kinds of recipes to submit, but also a ballpark figure for the number of ingredients and amount of space used for the method of preparation.

Submit recipes appropriate to the contest's focus. Don't send in a recipe for salad when the rules list the categories as hot breads, casseroles and desserts. One of the judging criteria is often appropriateness to the category.

Make sure that your recipe complies with the contest's ingredient rules. If you must use at least a cup of the sponsor's product, don't submit a recipe that calls for only three-fourths of a cup.

Check your eligibility to enter. Only people over 18 years of age (or under 18) can enter some contests. If you or a member of your family has owned beef cattle within a certain period of time, you cannot be a National Beef Cook-Off contestant. People in various occupations, such as chefs, food service professionals, or those who work for certain companies, are ineligible to enter other contests.

It's extremely important to pay attention to any judging criteria that may be mentioned in the contest announcement. Most common among them are taste, originality, creativity, ease of preparation, appearance, appropriate use of sponsor's product and availability of ingredients. Most major competitions stress originality. Rules for one of the big competitions, The National Chicken Cooking Contest, did not specify that recipes had to be original until after the 1991 competition, when the top winner received $25,000 for a recipe that was later discovered to have been printed in a 1989 issue of one of the leading food magazines.

The following were judging criteria for the 1991 contest as well as instructions to the judges:

1. TASTE (0-40 points)
   Does finished dish have flavor that will appeal to most people?
   Other ingredients should not overpower chicken.
   Seasonings and flavors should be strong enough to be tasty, but mild enough to seem palatable to the average person.
2. APPEARANCE (0-30 points)
   Does finished dish look appetizing?
   Garnishes and simple serving accompaniments such as rice or noodles are allowed.
   Whole chicken or any part or parts, soups, salads, etc. are all eligible; need not be identifiable as chicken.
   Just needs to look like something you would like to eat.
3. APPEAL (0-15 points)
   Is idea different enough to excite interest?

Is combination of ingredients a little different?
Is procedure somewhat innovative and unique and does it utilize interesting cooking methods?
Is general treatment of chicken a little unusual?
Does dish generally carry through with the highly nutritious value of chicken?
4. SIMPLICITY (0-15 points)
Is idea simple enough to appeal to most people?
Are ingredients familiar and readily available?
Are ingredients reasonably economical?
Is procedure simple enough that most people will want to try it?

Added to the rules for the 1993 contest (the competition is held in May of odd-numbered years) is a paragraph on originality. The originality requirement is spelled out at greater length than it is in the rules for most contests, but the intention is the same.

Entries must be original. "Original" is defined as not previously published in the same or substantially the same form. Contestant finalists will be required to certify that the recipe entry is "original."

It is most important to abide by the originality rule. Just changing bread crumbs to pieces of bread and 1 teaspoon black pepper to 1 teaspoon white pepper is not enough. Winners at various major competitions have had their prizes revoked when their entries were discovered to be copies of other recipes.

Opinions of experienced contesters vary as to what constitutes originality. According to some of them, it's okay to change only a couple of ingredients — substituting veal for chicken and spinach for carrots, for example — if by so doing you come up with an entirely different dish.

Others say it's cricket to take another recipe and alter the ingredients slightly but prepare it another way, i.e., broiling instead of poaching. Then, there's the technique of using the same ingredients but altering proportions substantially. As all cooks know, you can use the same ingredients to make muffins, cake, and cookies, but they're totally different products.

If you win one of the major prizes in a competition, you will usually be required to sign an affidavit (called affies by contesters) saying that your recipe has never been published.

When inclusion of a short statement about the recipe is not contrary to the rules and you can come up with a grabber, include it. Your blurb might be about the recipe's origin, versatility, thriftiness or nutritional value, such as "This dessert, ready to eat in minutes, is budget-easy, too."

Thousands of entries are received in the most prominent recipe contests, so you'll want to attract the judges' attention to set your recipe apart from the common submission. The most effective way to do so is to give your recipe a winning name. Be clever and upbeat, but never obscene. The name should tell something about the dish and make readers (judges) want to try it.

Luscious Lemon Mousse Pie, Chicken Salad with Cajun Dressing, Peacheasy Pie and King of Clubs Sandwich are four winning examples.

Although cleverness counts in some competitions, incorporating the featured food's name in a descriptive title is important in others. Here are the names of some winners in the Prune Festival Cook-Off, held each year in Yuba City, California: Prune and Pistachio Stuffed Chicken Breast, Prune Macadamia Clusters, Prune Sweet Potato Salad and French Prune and Pear Pie.

Putting the Ingredients Together (on Paper). Follow the contest rules exactly. If no directions for typing (or printing) the recipe are given, put your name and address, single spaced, in the upper left-hand corner. Center the recipe's title about four inches down on a page of 8½-by-11-inch plain white typing paper. Then list all the ingredients in the order they will be used. (I usually doublespace this part of the recipe.)

When commercial sponsors specify that a certain ingredient (or ingredients) must appear in the recipe, include the product with its full brand name in capital letters. In a contest sponsored by Quaker Oats Company, for example, you must identify the cornmeal as "QUAKER CORNMEAL." Products other than those manufactured by the sponsor are listed by their generic names (for example, "2 cups unbleached flour, 3 eggs, 1 teaspoon chopped fresh ginger"). If the sponsor produces other ingredients used in your recipe, call them by their brand names, even if they aren't the ingredient the contest is pushing. If you need proof that this technique helps, just read the entries published by companies (such as Kraft and Pillsbury) in any book of recipe contest winners.

I try to find recipes previously published by the sponsor to use as models when I'm typing preparation directions. However you type yours, keep them as clear and concise as you can and in the proper sequence. If the oven should be preheated, mention that at the beginning of the directions. Include appropriate pan, kettle or casserole sizes.

Don't forget to include all the necessary steps. In fact, it's a good idea to write down the directions at the same time you're actually preparing the dish. Following the directions, you might add information about a possible garnish: "Garnish with lemon peel spirals, if desired," for example. Close by giving the number of servings: "Serves 8-10."

Suggesting a garnish is especially important if the winning recipes must be prepared by their creators in a cook-off. In most cook-offs, the recipe must be prepared exactly as submitted. That means if you haven't mentioned a garnish, you can't garnish your entry at the competition.

WINNING WORDS

The way you work your words — in titles, blurbs and concise directions — can put your recipe entries at the head of the competition. Words *alone* can also win statement, limerick and naming contests.

It's more difficult to find out about these contests, since there's no publication devoted to them, although you will occasionally find them listed in *Blue Ribbon Cooks' Newsletter*. Since most of these contests are sponsored by the manufacturers of national brand products, they are usually announced (along with their rules and entry requirements) in magazine and Sunday newspaper supplement ads.

Since there are several devices that can be employed in all of these contest categories, let's talk about them before we discuss the contest types individually.

Acrostics. The first letter of each word or line spells another word, as in the following example.

> I like Finesse because "the old gray hair ain't what it used to be" until concentrated FINESSE "brings it back alive" naturally to *FINE* Silkiness, Sheen and youthful Elasticity. (underlining mine)

Alliteration. The use of two or more words beginning with the same letter, such as

> Pretty, Practical Playclothes that Please the Most Particular Pre-schooler.

Analogy. The adaptation of familiar terms from one field or subject to describe another. You might, for instance, use football terms in describing a breakfast cereal or movie jargon to sing the praises of a toothpaste.

Contrast. Using words with opposite meanings. For example:

> When I have to be bright and cheerful on a dark and gloomy day, I use Heads Up to head off the blues caused by sinus headaches.

Coined Words. Creating new words by combining, dividing, re-spelling, or otherwise changing traditional words. To me, this is one of the easiest devices to use and I used it to reasonable advantage in a contest that Carnation/Contadina sponsored a few years ago. It was a contest that everyone who looks through the food coupon inserts in the Sunday papers should have seen. And one that was fun to enter. The sponsor provided the first line of a four-line verse:

EAT AT HOME; IT REALLY PAYS . . .

All you had to do to win one of the ten grand prizes (refrigerator/freezer, range and dishwasher), fifty first prizes (microwave, black-and-white TV, coffeemaker and toaster oven) or one hundred second prizes (mixer/food processor/doughmaker/blender kitchen center) was to add three more lines that made a hit with the judges. I won one of the second prizes with this entry.

EAT AT HOME; IT REALLY PAYS
BOTH FOR CHOW-HOUNDS AND GOURMETS;
FOR COUCH SPUDS OR FOLKS ON THE RUN,
IT'S "CENTSIBLE" FOR EVERYONE.

Mystic Three. This is a phrase, coined years ago by Wilmer S. Shepherd, founder of the Shepherd School of Contesting, to define any interesting trio of words or phrases. We hear them every day, especially in songs and common expressions: baubles, bangles and beads; calm, cool and collected; ready, willing and able.

Shepherd maintained that employing this device—including three words or sets of words related to the contest theme—was one of the secrets of winning statement and jingle contests. After reading dozens of winning entries through the years, I'm convinced he was right.

Parody/paraphrase. Changing a well-known song, saying, quotation or the like, as in the "old gray hair" phrase in the foregoing acrostic example.

Repetition. Repeating the same or similar sounds, words or phrases:

More stylage, more mileage, more smileage.

Visual Tricks. The use of unusual punctuation, initials, abbreviations or upside-down words and phrases to catch the eye.

Other devices you might use are puns/plays on words or words with double meanings.

IN TWENTY-FIVE WORDS OR MORE

Statement contests go to almost any length to extol the virtues of a sponsor's product. The most common length requirement is for 25 words or less, but you will occasionally find entry rules asking for 50 or even 500.

If a 25- or 50-word statement is required, you'll no doubt wish you could use a few more. In 500-word statement contests, you may have shot your wad of hype when you've used only 400.

While using only 400 words in a 500-word statement contest won't disqualify you (you might even win if they are very well written), your advantage increases with the number of words you use to praise the sponsor's product.

Your statements need not be in prose. Verse is also popular with statement-contest judges. Of course, it's pretty hard to keep rhyming couplets until you've used up 500 words. But if the word length is from 25 to 50 words and rhyme comes easily for you, the form can be a winner.

FIVE-LINE RHYMES

In limerick contests, the first one, two or four lines are provided. It's up to the contestant to supply the rest. The limerick form has a standard rhyming pattern with no variations. There are always five lines, with the first, second and fifth lines rhyming with each other. The third and fourth lines (which are shorter than the others and indented) also rhyme with each other.

In composing your limerick entries, make lists of words appropriate to your subject. Next, with rhyming dictionary at hand, make more lists of words that rhyme with those in the first list.

If only the first line of the limerick is given, you have a single guiding rhyme word. Lines two and five must end in words with the same sound, but you're free to choose the words that will make your third and fourth lines rhyme. When four limerick lines are given, you need only come up with a punchy last line that rhymes with lines one and two.

For practice, let's say there's a contest sponsored by a magazine for writers, and the first line of the limerick is given: THERE ONCE WAS A WRITER NAMED BREEN.

Your first job will be to work on a rhyme list for the last word of the first line. Then you'll need to write down all the words and phrases you can think of that are associated with the writer's life: deadlines, novels, rejection, first drafts, research, interviews, poetry/poems/verse, articles/pieces, writer's block and so on. Take each of the words, write words that are, in turn, associated with them, and make more rhyme lists; for example, poetry—romantic, corny, sappy and so on.

If you're lucky, you'll find words on these lists that can be manipulated so that they rhyme with your first line list. Then, all you need to do is to create two other lines (the third and fourth) that make sense.

Your first results, like mine, probably won't be that terrific, but you will have an idea of how the process works and have lots of fun, too.

> THERE ONCE WAS A WRITER NAMED BREEN
> WHOSE LIMERICKS WEREN'T VERY CLEAN
> HIS MEANINGS, THOUGH DOUBLE,
> WEREN'T THE CAUSE OF THE TROUBLE;
> 'TWAS THE PAUSES HE LEFT IN BETWEEN.

NAMING NAMES

Contests that utilize the coined word technique to the fullest require the entrant to create a name for a product or a character (usually product "mascots" such as the butler pictured on Lunch Bucket products). Most winners create these names from product characteristics or by using words that are spelled differently but sound the same or have other meanings.

Rosemary Berger, who lives in North Carolina, did just that for her winning entry—Justin X. Grape—in Sunmaid's "Name the Raisins" contest.

MAGAZINE MAIL-INS

Magazine contests are a mixed bag. Among the regulars are the kid's saying ($25), joke ($10) and captioned photo ($100) contests in each issue of *Woman's World*. Naming the place featured in a photograph and puzzles of various sorts are among the other kinds of contests you'll find.

As we mentioned earlier, recipe contests in high-visibility magazines pay big prizes. There are other kinds of competitions in these publications as well. Some of them appear in the editorial copy and others in the ads. These contests range from essay competitions to those seeking the best gingerbread houses, decorated Easter eggs or Santa Claus cookies.

WINNING WAYS

Rosemary Berger says that whenever she begins working on an entry for any kind of contest, she buys the sponsoring organization's product and analyzes it, whether it be toothpaste or tomatoes. She also analyzes any messages the sponsor uses in promoting the competition.

Savvy 30-Minute Writers will follow Berger's example. It isn't necessary to use sponsored products regularly to compete in their contests, but it is important to become familiar with the product's uses, ingredients, and features touted in its ads.

Before you begin composing your entries, list words and phrases describing the product. For example, suppose you want to enter a statement contest focusing on a certain brand of hand cream. Your list might look something like this:

> all natural ingredients
> doesn't feel greasy
> comes in two scents (fresh lime and apricot)
> there also is odorless variety
> comes in easy-to-hold jar
> jar is a pretty shade of pink slightly darker than cream
> cover fits firmly, but comes off without difficulty
> less expensive than other brands

makes hands smoother in a few days
safe for children's skin

It's important during this part of your research to note as much as you can about the product's smell, texture, appearance and taste (if applicable, of course).

Next, copy down the ingredients, underlining any that are unusual or that set the product apart from its competitors and might be considered selling points: natural flavorings, rare fragrances, added nutrition. Sometimes you'll want to note ingredients that are missing: preservatives, fat, salt, abrasives and other undesirables.

Then study the product's advertisements in newspapers and magazines or on television and radio. Read everything written on the container to promote the product. What aspects of the product are the sponsors/ad agencies promoting? Are any of the words or phrases candidates for wordplays? Who are the potential purchasers: home owners, children, the general public, athletes? Can you think of clever, alternative uses for the product? List phrases the advertisers have chosen to herald the product's attributes. Also study any contest newsletters that contain tips on the contest or others somewhat like it.

Start writing when you have analyzed your subject thoroughly. Don't worry about word length until later. If you have done your homework well, you will have more material than you can possibly use—and plenty of ammunition if you want to fire off more than one entry.

After you have spent twenty or thirty minutes consciously matching up information with ideas and devices, push everything into your subconscious and go about some other task. It's amazing how often inspiration surfaces while you're weeding the petunias, putting new spark plugs in the car, feeding the cat, or working on another writing project.

THE CONTESTER'S REFERENCE SHELF

Many of the reference books you will want for contesting are those you already have in your writing library: a dictionary, a thesaurus, a rhyming dictionary and a book of quotations. You'll also find that books of limericks, jokes, proverbs, famous poems, fairy tales and even nursery rhymes are useful. An oldie as far as contest books are concerned — but a goodie when it comes to thousands of homonyms, rhymes, and double-meaning words — is *Prize Winning Jingles*, by William Sunners. It's available at some libraries and is a wonderful investment for contesters who can find copies at used book stores.

You can sometimes obtain copies of a contest's winning entries by sending an SASE to the address provided in a contest's rules. Serious contesters send for this information whenever it is available. Winning entries are great for starting the associative process when you're entering similar contests. They're even more worthwhile when you enter a subsequent contest by the same sponsor.

Although it isn't unusual for some contestants to send as many as one hundred entries to the big-prize contests, this strikes me as overkill. If you do submit multiple entries, experienced contesters suggest that you use a different version of your name on each of them so that you can identify your winning entry. In most cases, judging agencies or sponsors will inform you only that you've won a prize, without alluding to the content of the entry itself.

Another good technique when sending multiple entries is to stagger the mailing dates. Since the judging process is highly subjective, you don't want all your entries to land at the same time on the desk of a judge who has a terrible backache.

To decide which contests to enter, assess your interests and skills, the amount of time you will have to spend, and whether or not you consider the prize worthwhile. Frankly, I'd rather win a lifetime supply of computer disks than a mink coat.

GETTING READY FOR JUDGMENT DAY

Knowing how the contest judging process works will help you as a competitor. As a general rule, all entries are picked up in mail sacks from the post office to which they are addressed, then transported to the prescreening organization or to the judging agency.

The prescreening is sometimes the job of an accounting firm (as is the case in the Pillsbury Bake-Off) though more typically it's done by the public relations firm or other agency, such as a chamber of commerce, that is conducting the contest. Some contests, such as that put on each year by Bays English Muffins, are run entirely by the company sponsoring them.

Once the entries are received, the first step in the process involves passing them through envelope-slitting machines and checking for any qualifiers (box tops, UPCs, labels or other proofs of purchase) the contest rules may require. Entries without the requisite qualifiers are thrown out. So are illegible submissions and those postmarked after the contest's closing date.

There are other rule violations: typed or written entries when hand-printing has been specified; failing to include one's name and address (or the dealer's name if that is required); exceeding the number of words allowed; using less than the stated amount of the sponsor's product as required in recipe contest rules. In short, adding or deleting anything not specified in the rules can result in disqualification.

It has been estimated that 60 to 70 percent of all contest entries are thrown out unread because rules have been broken. Estimates from some people who conduct contests go even higher, to as many as 95 percent.

The survivors—entries from people who have followed the rules to the letter—go on to preliminary readers who do more winnowing, casting out entries that are profane, obscene, or just don't make sense. Then the lower-echelon judges take over and rate the remaining entries according to criteria established for the contest. Originality and creativity, appropriateness, sincerity and clarity are the usual judging criteria in statement, limerick and naming contests. Typical for recipe contests are originality, availability of ingredients, appropriate use of sponsor's product, appearance, taste and ease of preparation. Although how various criteria are weighted differs with each contest, originality is almost always one of the most important considerations.

At this stage, duplicate (or very similar) entries hit the wastebaskets. The remaining entries, with the junior judges' scores attached to them, go on to the judging agency's (or sponsors') top executives for final judging.

Your entry can get past most of its competition if you simply follow the rules. I always highlight or underline them so I won't miss any. The following checklist will help you, too.

1. Is the entry to be typed, printed or written?
2. What size paper is called for?
3. Must an official entry blank be included? Can the original entry blank be photocopied?
4. Should the completed entry form be attached to the entry or not?
5. What qualifiers (if any) should be enclosed?
6. Is the way qualifiers should be attached specified?
7. Is your name and address to go on the same sheet as the entry or on a separate piece of paper?
8. Is the envelope size specified? (If no size is specified, use a business envelope.)
9. Must you sign your entry or entry blank? (Be sure not to print if a signature is called for.)
10. Is the envelope addressed correctly? If, for example, rules give the following address:

Sally's "Saucey Salad Dressing" Contest
P.O. Box 777, Dept. EZ
Washington, D.C. 12345

Don't forget the quotation marks and don't spell out words that are abbreviated. Be sure the post office box and zip code numbers are correct, and don't leave out the department letters. If the envelope's information varies *in any way* from that specified, your entry may not even be opened before it is discarded.

THE 30-MINUTE WRITER'S PLAN OF ACTION

1. On an inexpensive or "give-away" calendar used only for contesting, write the names of contests you would like to enter on the months when their deadlines occur.

2. Set up a file for each contest, adding magazine/newspaper recipes that you might change and adapt. Go through cookbooks for ideas, too.

3. Experiment in the kitchen. Make one basic dish and divide it into fourths, using different flavorings/techniques for each portion. If the recipe's basis is a cake mix or cookie batter, you might even be able to divide it into sixths. That way, you'll be able to do a maximum amount of experimenting with a minimum amount of work and cost.

4. Eliminate the so-so dishes; refine those that show promise, using the divide-and-experiment technique.

5. Neatly prepare your entries, paying close attention to the rules. Send them off, and start dreaming up entries for the next contest.

CHAPTER XIII
Kid Stuff

Three writers I know were sitting around one day, talking about writers whose work they admired. The name of one, whose byline you would recognize immediately, came up—only to be dismissed with a disparaging "but he sells to children's magazines."

What these writers—all of whom write for the medium-pay markets—didn't realize is that the object of their scorn was making more for his pieces in *Sports Illustrated for Kids* and *Highlights for Children* than they were for the articles they sold to *Newsday* and *Cruise Travel Magazine*—and writing about half the words.

This is not to say that all children's publications pay princely (or princessly) amounts. Many of them pony up only two or three cents a word, just like some publications for adults. But the fact that top children's magazines pay very good rates helps set to rest the myth that writing for youngsters is somehow easier than writing for adults.

As a matter of fact, writing for children requires a special talent, that of being able to put yourself into a child's mind, to remember how you felt when you were four or eight or eleven. And you'll need to be able to say what you need to in few words, as kiddie articles are rarely more than 900 words in length.

You also have to be a translator of sorts, substituting the feelings and curiosities you had as a youngster for those of today's children. Although children who grew up before the advent of space shuttles and test-tube babies had the same basic emotions youngsters have today, they grew up in different environments and therefore had different experiences.

My mother pointed this out to me some years ago when her grandsons were worrying aloud about the threat of nuclear war. "When I was little," Mom said, "we worried about the horse running away with the buggy. That could mean death, too." Yesterday's child cried over a broken china doll. Today's child, with a doll made of state-of-the-art plastic, cries when the mechanism that makes the doll talk won't work anymore. But they both shed the same tears.

Most of all, you must be excited by the concept of writing for kids. Children are enthusiastic and haven't had time to become jaded, blasé or disillusioned. And they don't want to read pieces by writers who have.

FIRST STEPS

If you think you have the qualifications for putting together children's pieces, you'll find that they fit in well with your life as a 30-Minute Writer. For one thing, researching the markets takes less time than for adult nonfiction since there are far fewer publications for kids.

When you begin your market research, you may have only a single publication in mind. However, the more options you have, the greater your potential for sales. So you'll want to expand your list of possibilities.

Best place to start is by studying the pages of the current *Children's Writer's & Illustrator's Market* (Writer's Digest Books). The juvenile section of *Writer's Market* also lists about two dozen publications.

Remember, though, that some adult publications also use a limited amount of material for children. Ten percent of the material in *Single Parent* is aimed at youngsters; 3 percent in *Cat Fancy*. Several of the leading women's magazines, such as *Family Circle* and *Good Housekeeping*, occasionally have children's pages, especially for Christmas, Easter and other special days.

You'll notice that in magazine listings, children are divided into age groups. One of the most common divisions is two- to five-year-olds, six- to eight-year-olds, and nine- to twelve-year-olds. Thirteen- to nineteen-year-olds are considered teens or young adults. Another system describes children aged five to eight as young readers, those nine to eleven as middle readers, and those twelve and up as young adults (feature articles for people in this latter group are often as long as those in adult magazines and so usually aren't 30-Minute Writer material).

Be on the lookout for publications aimed at children wherever you go—at your friends' homes, dentists' offices, newsstands. Beg, borrow or buy those that interest you. Check the children's magazines at your local library, too. Many libraries allow card holders to check them out just like books.

Chances are, you won't be able to find half the publications you find listings for. But don't give up. You can send for sample copies of those publications that sound promising. Some of them will cost two or three dollars, but most only require a self-addressed stamped 8-by-11-inch envelope.

KEEPING TRACK OF THE MARKETS

While holding the image of a single magazine in your mind is simple, trying mentally to catalog a half dozen is tough. Therefore, as you study the markets, develop a method for keeping track.

For example, you can make asterisks in the margins next to those you think you might want to write for, underlining or highlighting important information—the publication's address, editor's name, rate of pay, whether payment is on acceptance or publication, word length, the kinds of material used—so you'll be able to find it at a glance. Or you might want to clip (or photocopy) the covers, contents pages and mastheads of your target magazines and make separate files. Whenever you find pertinent information and articles that you think might be helpful patterns to follow when you begin to write, add the material to your files.

As you study the magazines, it won't take long to realize that, like adult magazines, publications for children have distinctive personalities. What it is difficult for some would-be writers to understand is that unless they come up with ideas compatible to those personalities, no letters of acceptance will pop into their mailboxes.

Your number one priority, therefore, as a children's magazine analyst, is to get a personality profile of each publication you hope to write for. There are several ways to get the information you need.

Most kiddie magazines have tag lines after their names, and if you want to make full use of your writing time, you'll spend the seconds necessary to read them. *Boys' Life*, for example, is subtitled "The Magazine for All *Boys*" (italics mine). Some girls may enjoy reading its articles, but the magazine definitely isn't one in which you'll make an editorial hit if you pull out all your nonsexist stops. *Noah's Ark*, subtitled "A Newspaper for Jewish Children," gives you information at the outset that all material should be suitable for Jewish youngsters — no kids eating nonkosher hot dogs or doing anything else contrary to Judaic law.

Cobblestone, with its subhead, "The history magazine for young people," focuses each issue on some period or aspect of history such as the Santa Fe Trail, the French and Indian Wars or the Cold War. Information on historically oriented films and books, quizzes and crossword puzzles are also featured in the magazine.

You might think that *Cricket*'s subtitle, "The magazine for children," isn't much of an enlightener. And you're right . . . to a degree. However, the broader the subtitle, the more general a magazine's content. By contrast, *Stone Soup* has the subtitle, "The Magazine *by* Children" (italics mine). This means that as an adult you have positively no hope of selling to the publication.

Instead of subtitles, other juvenile publications have a line of small print on the cover that indicates the sponsoring organization. For example, *Ranger Rick* is published monthly by the National Wildlife Federation, while *Zillions* is produced by Consumers Union. It would be extremely unusual if an article written for one of these publications would fit into the other.

Contact, published by the Children's Television Network, is one of the kiddies' publications I find most interesting. Articles include the likes of "Stones and Bones" (on Neanderthal Man) and "Things to Come" (predictions for the future, such as advances in organic gardening). Included in a regular department called "Factoids" are tidbits such as "Slugs have four noses," "There are 193 different kinds of monkeys," and "Boys are more likely to catch colds than girls."

National Geographic World, as you might expect, features the same sorts of subjects you'll find in *National Geographic*, only they're geared to youngsters. Heavy on environment and natural history, it answers questions like "How do robins know where to find worms?" "How do erasers work?" and "Why do butterflies fly mostly on sunny days?" But you would be making a mistake if you thought of only natural history and the environment when gathering article ideas for the magazine, for along with a preponderance of articles with titles like "Reaching Out to Raptors," there's an occasional piece like "Roller Power" about blading (skating on in-line roller skates).

Targeting isn't quite as precise when you're writing for children's publications sponsored by various religions—at least as far as the general subject matter is concerned. But specifics in your article must be tailored to fit those religions' philosophies. *Wonder* is published weekly by the Church of the Nazarene. *Friend* is the weekly publication of the Church of Jesus Christ of the Latter-Day Saints. And *High Adventure* (for boys) is published by the Assemblies of God.

IT PAYS TO BE INFORMED

Each little bit of information you get about a magazine may not mean a lot in itself, but by putting the bits together, the personality emerges. By reading the information in market listings of children's magazines, for example, you'll learn that the National Wildlife Federation's *Ranger Rick* describes itself as a "monthly magazine for children from ages 6 to 12, with the greatest concentration in the 7 to 10 bracket."

By scanning the magazine, you find that each issue contains articles about animals, reptiles and birds. Sometimes, one species is the focus of most of an issue; at other times a variety of creatures are written about. Your research will also show you that *Ranger Rick* is one of the highest paying of the children's magazines, with rates of from $50 to $550 depending on length, quality and content. Considering that the maximum article length is 900 words, that can amount to impressive money.

Unfortunately, you'll find that most kiddie mags don't pay that much. It's difficult to make any generalizations about the amounts that children's magazines send to their contributors, however. As with adult publications, frequent contributors get more for their work than first-time writers. Payment can range from two or three cents a word upward, with publications sponsored by religious organizations usually paying the lower rates. Eight to ten cents per word is typical for publications such as *Children's Digest* and *Children's Playmate Magazine*.

I simply cannot emphasize too strongly that if you want to succeed, you'll spend all the thirty-minute sessions it takes to get as much information as possible about the magazines you would like to sell to. For example, suppose you decide to aim for publication in *Boys' Life*, which is sponsored by the Boy Scouts of America.

According to the listing in *Writer's Market*, the magazine "pays minimum $500 for major article text" (preferred length 1,500 words) and "Much better rates if you really know how to write for your market." In that listing, under "Tips," the *Boys' Life* people say, "We strongly recommend reading at least 12 issues of the magazine and learning something about the programs of the Boy Scouts of America before you submit queries. We are a good market for any writer willing to do the necessary homework."

If the people who edit a magazine make recommendations, writers looking for sales had better heed them. Though the suggested publication research takes three or four thirty-minute segments of writing time, it's well worth the effort.

You will quickly see, for example, that most issues of *Boys'*

Life contain six or seven feature articles, usually a couple of them with a direct tie-in to scouting. Subject matter is extremely diverse (remember the magazine is for boys whose age range spans ten years). Bicycling, cars, fishing, ecology, entertainment, health, hobbies, movies, magic, pets and science are only a sampling of the subjects written about.

But more important than the breadth of subject matter is knowing that whether the subject is a famous sports star or Komodo dragons, *Boys' Life* topics are always presented with an air of adventure. "Mystery of the Lost Dutchman Mine Lives On" and "Riding America's Wildest Roller Coasters" are typical of the article titles.

This sort of information is worth a lot when you begin to sort out your idea possibilities. Some topics naturally have a sense of excitement about them. Others are interesting, perhaps, but without innate punch. You'll realize that you should go with the former for *Boys' Life* and reserve the others for markets that use more passive material.

INCREASING YOUR ODDS

By using effective information-gathering techniques, you'll put yourself giant steps ahead of the competition; you will not only be zeroing in on editor-approved copy, but also on a broader target area.

For example, you'll learn by reading the fine print that the Children's Better Health Institute of the Benjamin Franklin Literary & Medical Society, Inc. (the same nonprofit foundation that puts out the *Saturday Evening Post*), publishes *Turtle Magazine for Preschool Kids* (for ages 2-5), *Humpty Dumpty's Magazine* (4-6), *Children's Playmate Magazine* (6-8), *Jack and Jill* (7-9), *Child Life* (9-11) and *Children's Digest* (10-13).

This multiplicity of publications under one umbrella can be an advantage. The magazines receive about a thousand submissions a month. If your idea or article is a good one but not quite right for the magazine to which you've sent it, the editor will pass it along to editors of affiliated publications who might be better able to use it.

Although good manuscripts get passed around, most submissions don't make the cut. According to Elizabeth Rinck, who edits both *Children's Digest* and *Children's Playmate*, many writers who submit material may understand that about one-third of the content of each magazine deals specifically with health/safety, but they don't seem to realize that whatever the topic, good health and safety practices cannot be ignored.

Rinck says, "Lots of people think 'I'll write for kids for practice.' They don't realize that you have to work just as hard—or harder—writing for children." She goes on to say that she sees "too many encyclopedic articles that regurgitate information that's available elsewhere."

To be sure that your material is fresh, gather it through interviews rather than books. Instead of recycling information from articles and books, contact the authors (through their publishers) if you can and ask them if they've come up with anything new on their subjects. Enlist the help of local experts. It's true that you'll occasionally have to rely on previously published material for facts and your background information, but do everything you can to keep that information from sounding like "the same old boring stuff."

"Another frequent mistake made by writers is trying to teach too much. There's not enough entertainment and fun," Rinck says. To discover the ratio of instruction/entertainment your editor favors, it's necessary to study the publication she puts together. As you analyze the articles, you'll see that the editors' ideas are not always the same on this balance, even though their magazines are aimed at the same age groups.

LITTLE IDEAS MEAN BIG SALES

After you've spent several thirty-minute sessions reading kiddie mags, your idea machine should begin whirring. If kids like to read about what British children learn in school, it computes that they would probably like to read about what Finnish children do during vacation. As you turn a magazine's pages, all sorts of similar associations will come to mind.

To add to your supply of juvenile article ideas, you'll want to consult the experts: Talk to the kids themselves.

Find out what latest fads, games, programs and teenage idols are considered cool. And speaking of cool, listen to their language. Although there's overlap, different words are popular among the various age groups.

Talk to people at places where children like to go—theme parks, zoos, recreation departments, children's libraries. Find out what the kids like best to do there.

Make a list of the articles in back issues of your targeted publication that sound most like those you would like to write, then start substituting words in the titles. "All about Seagulls" could become "All about Eagles" or "All about Pelicans." One athlete's battle against drugs could become another athlete's battle against a near-crippling injury.

Look through your adult article idea file. Contrary to what the writers in the first paragraph of this chapter think, a good many top writers of adult material—Isaac Asimov, among others—also write for youngsters. It's a great way to make your research do double duty.

Walter L. Roessing, a prolific producer of adult fiction, also writes for *Boys' Life* and other scouting publications. Roessing got the idea for "Big League Bat Boys" at a spring training game in Palm Springs when his thirteen-year-old son said, as he watched the bat boys, "Gee, that would be fun."

Roessing, who has written articles about the biggest players in pro football and the smallest players in professional basketball, tries to find "unusual angles that everyone is aware of but doesn't think of as articles." He says, "When I see an unusual statistic in *USA Today*, I do a little research to see if it will work as a piece."

MOST SALABLE SUBJECTS

Children's pieces fall into three major categories: 1.) biographies/profiles, 2.) informational articles about processes, events, and the creatures—both plant and animal—that inhabit the world around us and 3.) how-tos.

Most biographies are about famous historical characters who have made outstanding contributions to society: Teddy Roosevelt, Marie Curie, Albert Schweitzer. Profiles usually are of children who have accomplished something out of the ordinary, like a twelve-year-old with a thriving mail-order business, or adults whose exploits, inventions, accomplishments or jobs are of interest to youngsters.

When you're thinking of children to profile, keep in mind that, while the little child likes to hear stories about children "just my size," elementary school children almost always want to read about kids who are older than—or at least not younger than—they are.

The most popular subjects for informationals are related to science (both natural and physical), health, animals, sports, hobbies and people/places in other lands. When writing any informational piece, keep the journalist's who, when, what, why and how firmly in mind. *Especially* the why. Kids ask a lot of questions, and you'll want to anticipate all of them.

Asking yourself questions is one of the best ways to come up with ideas. How do salmon find the streams where they were hatched? Why does bread rise? Where do clowns shop for their clothes?

Don't neglect topics formerly considered of interest only to adults: pollution, war, international relations, nuclear power, divorce, even death. Children watch adult TV programs and the news. They're concerned as well as curious about what they see.

Articles written on levels appropriate to a child's skills, maturity and emotions can help a lot to sort things out.

How-to subjects for children's articles run the gamut from making new friends to planning a Valentine's Day party to catching a turtle and training it to race. Advice in these pieces is straightforward, practical and uncomplicated. It's important in generating how-to ideas that they be relevant both to the readers' lives and the magazine's focus.

There are exceptions. Take the turtle training piece, for instance. A child living in Manhattan doesn't have much chance of raising a turtle, let alone catching one. But that child might love to read the article because he can dream that "maybe someday. . . ."

RESEARCH REMINDERS

You can't spin children's pieces off the top of your head. And as Elizabeth Rinck points out, "Just because you're writing for an audience that doesn't know everything yet, don't think you can be sloppy about research." Unlike skeptical adults, children tend to believe everything they read. Therefore, writers of informational articles for youngsters have to be particularly scrupulous about the accuracy of their facts.

This doesn't mean that your fact finding has to be hard work. Although author Ann Boyle usually writes juvenile fiction, her research advice makes good sense for writers of juvenile nonfiction as well. "I like to start my research with books from the children's section of the library," she says, "because they don't have more information than you need. Also, they're easier to understand. And if you need more information, you can easily go to the adult section."

However you obtain your information, the pros recommend getting a good foundation in the subject you're writing about. Then after you've written the article, they advise that you find someone who is well-versed in your subject to review the manuscript before it is sent to the publisher.

When interviewing a subject for a profile, children's writers use many of the same techniques that writers of adult personality pieces do. But there's an additional ingredient that good writers look for: some human trait that children can relate to. If he had a hard time with arithmetic in school, if her father has to remind her to do the chores, if he frets because he isn't as big as the other kids his age, tell your readers.

Don't portray your profile personality as perfect. Your readers must be able to identify in some way with the person written about, to see that person as someone who, despite accomplishments, is a human being rather than a god or goddess they can never hope to emulate.

STAYING IN STYLE

When you begin writing, remember that being a copycat is okay as far as style is concerned. In fact, it's essential if you want to please the editor. It's especially important to keep your sentences of the same length as those in previously published articles.

Choose words of the same degree of difficulty, too. To find out if you're writing at the proper reading level, have a person who teaches children of the targeted ages read over your manuscript.

Since articles for preschool or elementary-school-aged children are most often from 400 to 600 words, you will soon realize that there's no space for any literary pyrotechnics. Don't waste time thinking of phrases to show that you have a way with words. Just say it as it is.

Sentences, you'll find, are almost always simply declarative or interrogative. They're short and to the point. Quotes are, too. Statistics, when used, are easy to understand. And be especially careful that figures of speech (metaphors, similes and personification) are in sync with the children's experience levels.

There's a tendency among children's writers who produce rejected manuscripts to preach or moralize, to tell instead of show. Even in the fundamentalist publications for youngsters, the emphasis is on teaching by example.

As work on your manuscript progresses, keep asking yourself the following questions. You might not get "yes" answers to all of them. That's okay. But if you don't get any positive responses, you had better not consider the article ready to submit until you do.

1. Is the subject exciting?
2. Does the article entertain as well as inform?
3. Will it capture readers' imaginations?
4. Will it trigger their curiosities, make them want to learn more about the subject?
5. Will it influence behavior positively?

PICTURE PERFECT

Although many children's articles are illustrated by drawings, good photos can often make the difference between a sale and a near-miss. Your best guides to the kinds of pictures you should submit with the manuscript are those photos the art directors have chosen for past issues of the magazine.

As you study the pictures, ask yourself questions like: Are they action shots? Are there people in the pictures? How many people are usually pictured? What sorts of clothes are they wearing? From what distance are the photos taken (close-ups, overview shots of events or scenery)? And, of course, pay particular attention to whether the photos are in color, in black and white, or if both are used.

CHILDREN'S ACTIVITIES

Requiring fewer words but more creativity than articles are those equally important activity pages that you find in just about every kiddie magazine. Most of these activities fall into seven categories: crafts, experiments, jokes, puzzles, quizzes, recipes and riddles.

Ideas for children's activities come fastest to people whose own activities include doing puzzles, laughing at jokes and working on crafts. But even if your days are too busy for these pastimes, you can generate ideas by browsing through activity books. Adapt those that children would be capable of completing, changing them so that they center on subjects or items that interest youngsters.

By simplifying adult-item craft projects, you'll devise articles that ten years ago were titled "Presents for Mother's (or Father's) Day." But since many of today's families aren't traditional, you might want to call such craft projects "Gifts for Grown-Ups You Like."

Children also love to make items they can use to decorate their bikes, their books, their rooms or themselves. Study grown-up fashion and decorating trends, or take ideas that were popular several years (or decades) ago and update them.

Since children's publications pay a great deal of attention to the seasons, you might want to list special days or times of year, noting activities and objects associated with each. Under "Winter" your list of possibilities could include:

Word scramble based on winter sports and activities (skis, sleds, etc.)

Craft project: making pom-poms for ice skates

Recipe: variation of hot chocolate or other cold-weather drink; cake or ice cream dessert shaped like snowballs

Minicrosswords built around winter themes (icicles, snowshoes, mittens, etc.)

Putting together your first children's article or activity is not going to be child's play, and the payment for that first piece may only amount to piggy bank money. But as you continue to refine your skills, you'll have to spend far fewer thirty-minute sessions to complete each piece.

You can spend the time you save going to the bank with those bigger and more frequent checks.

THE 30-MINUTE WRITER'S PLAN OF ACTION

1. Read a half-dozen kiddies' magazines to see if you really enjoy the kinds of material they contain. If the pieces are fun for you to read, chances are you'll like writing them as well.

2. Spend your next sessions compiling mini-dossiers on your targeted publications.

3. Start manufacturing ideas. Write down each one that crosses your mind, no matter how silly it may seem. Ideas have a way of metamorphosing into better ones if you give them a chance.

4. Before you query the editor, notice whether he or she likes the tight focus or prefers a survey approach to subjects.

5. When you start to write, pay attention to word length in previously published pieces. How many words of more than two syllables, for example, do you find in a 600-word piece?

Don't make your article any more complicated than those that have gone before it.

Above all, don't let your tone sound like you're addressing a bunch of junior eggheads. Forget the miniversions of adult scholarly publications.

Whenever I read one of these children's articles I think of a little boy I once saw wearing a scaled-down tuxedo. It may have fit size-wise, but psychologically it didn't seem to fit at all.

6. Package your product professionally. And if it comes bouncing back, be like a feisty kid. Jump up, brush yourself off, make some minor revisions so it will fit another publication and send the piece out again in the next mail.

CHAPTER XIV

Itty-Bitty Stories

King Shahayar reclined against his pillows of silk and brocade, unable to sleep. Since his wife's betrayal, he had ordered his chief minister to bring him a virgin each night. Each morning he had ordered that same minister to slay his companion in order to ensure her fidelity. When there were no more maidens in the kingdom, his bride of the night was the daughter of the chief minister. She had persuaded her father to lay her virginity and life at the foot of the insatiable ruler, for she had a plan.

"I will tell you a little story," she said. And so strong was the spell she wove that she was not killed on the morrow as more than a thousand of her predecessors had been. Nor did she die after the thousandth night, or after the thousandth and first.

The editor examined the chip in her nail polish and wondered why she had let her secretary book an appointment with this freelancer from Boondocksville. After all, she'd never bought an article from an unknown and she doubted she ever would. The freelancer was aware of her policy. But he had a plan.

"Let me tell you a little story," he said.

The editor, heretofore known to her staff as the Great Stone Face, heard the story and erupted in laughter that shook the outer office filing cabinets and echoed down to the water cooler in the hall. The writer got his assignment—and another, and another.

ANECDOTES: LITTLE STORIES FOR LARGE SUMS

Writers use anecdotes as tools in writing full-length articles and books. These miniature stories can provide leads (as did the foregoing anecdote), offer glimpses into a personality, increase the credibility of informational articles, and dramatize points in problem how-tos.

For the 30-Minute Writer, the anecdote is more than a device. It's an end in itself, and one worth pursuing because it answers the most common complaint among busy would-be writers: "I might be able to find time to write, but never the hours it takes for research." Happily for them, anecdotes usually don't require any research at all.

An anecdote is a short story, simply told, with a beginning, middle and end. It is a little story—usually 200 to 500 words long—based on an actual happening, a short account or retelling of a single incident. To be successful, it must evoke a feeling on the part of the reader: laughter, surprise, sympathy, or some other emotional reaction.

As a miniversion of a story, the anecdote is expected to provide enough information to allow us to picture the event it describes, but we aren't looking for detailed explanations of how the principals look or why they behave as they do. The following anecdote by Bennett Cerf shows how a few well-chosen words can fulfill our expectations:

> The story goes that Mrs. Vanderbilt once demanded to know what Fritz Kreisler would charge to play at a private musicale, and was taken aback when he named a price of five thousand dollars. She agreed reluctantly, but added, "Please remember that I do not expect you to mingle with the guests." "In that case, Madam," Kreisler assured her, "my fee will be only two thousand."

Note the strong, descriptive verbs, *demanded*, *taken aback*, *assured*; the adverb, *reluctantly*; the hauteur conveyed by word placement in "Please remember that I do not expect you . . ."; and the marvelous put-down expressed in the closing retort.

STORY SOURCES

Many ideas for anecdotes come out of our own experiences.

If you stop to think about it, life is often a series of little stories that the alert writer can capitalize upon.

Conversations (including those that are overheard) are another productive source of ideas. I don't know about you, but friends are always telling me about the funny thing that happened on the way to work, the strange encounter a nephew had, or the cute remark a grandchild made. Eavesdropping may not be considered polite, but you'll hear some great stories that way, too.

It's important to remember that the people who regularly sell anecdotes haven't had any more experiences than the average person. They have, however, learned to identify experiences that make good stories and to craft them professionally.

Not all incidents can be fashioned into anecdotes. In order to work, the incident must have at least one of the following attributes: humor (the biggest seller), drama/tension, conflict/complication, an inherent lesson or a surprise ending or twist. Most good anecdotes contain more than one of these ingredients.

By way of illustration, here's an anecdote based on an incident that happened several years ago.

> Christmastime was approaching and we wanted to share the season's joy with others. Since we had just moved to town, I asked a school nurse who attended our church if she knew of some child who most likely wouldn't receive any Christmas presents.
>
> Two days later, she phoned to tell us about a boy in seventh grade named Jeff, who lived with his mother in a run-down trailer court. Jeff, she said, wanted an alarm clock for Christmas.

(Note: although the choice of gift is unusual, so far there's nothing remarkable about such a scenario. No drama, no surprises.)

> About two weeks after Christmas, we saw the school nurse at Sunday services and asked her if Jeff was pleased with his gift.

"Oh, he was pleased all right," she said. "But he didn't keep the clock. Never intended to. Gave it to his best friend, Matt, who's always in trouble being late for school.

"You should have seen Jeff when he told me about it," she continued. "Grinned from ear to ear. 'It was the first time I ever had a present to give to anybody,' he said."

Notice how effectively the surprise ending brings the little story to a close, evoking emotional response galore.

FACTS OR FABRICATION

Prospective anecdote writers often ask how faithfully they must relate the story. Must they set it down as it really happened? This question isn't easy to answer. Actual events, however dramatic or humorous or exciting they may be, don't always have the same qualities when transferred to paper. There are times when facts must be slightly altered or the time frame compressed to make the story work in print. Quotes may have to be rearranged for maximum impact, to clean up the language, or for a dozen other reasons.

Time frame problems usually occur when a story unfolds gradually over weeks, months or even years. The story becomes too drawn out if each event is related in turn. Instead, you must condense some incidents so that the reader gets a clear picture of what happened without becoming bogged down in unnecessary detail. Instead of chronicling every symptom a disappointed child displayed, for example, you might synopsize: "During the months that followed, Sarah rushed to the mailbox every day after school, becoming so distraught that her parents considered talking to the school psychologist."

I know a writer whose children were twenty-two and twenty years old when she sold an anecdote based on an event that took place fifteen years before. In relating the event, she referred to her seven-year-old daughter and five-year-old son. If it didn't bother her kids, I can see no problem with that kind of fact-changing.

On the other hand, I do have trouble accepting completely

fabricated anecdotes. Besides, if you have ever tried to create a story out of thin air, you know it's almost impossible.

There is, I realize, a vast gulf between a small point of fact and total fabrication. But as far as this middle ground is concerned, however much is changed must depend upon the individual writer. My personal rule is that minor and cosmetic changes are okay, but changes in the substantive truth are not, since there are readers who believe that everything they read — including anecdotal material — is true.

Another reason for changing words around is that people don't usually say things in a way that makes for sparkling anecdote dialogue. They leave out words, sprinkle their speech with *okays* and *you knows*, dangle participles, and use plural verb forms with singular nouns. Then, too, people emphasize words with their voices rather than the way they place them in sentences.

Therefore, a spoken sentence that brings laughs can be a dud on paper. It's up to you, the writer, to work with the words until they provide the zing your anecdote needs.

However much you alter what really happened, you must succeed in making the story "read true." Readers, however unsophisticated, know when they are being put on. How much juggling you do depends, in the long run, on your code of journalism ethics and your ability to fabricate convincingly.

ANECDOTE ANALYSIS

Anecdotes are written from two points of view: first person and third person. Two factors determine the point of view you should use: the style of your intended publication and the material with which you are working.

The principal devices employed in writing anecdotes are narration, description, imagery and dialogue.

Narration. Narration is simply the act of telling, or narrating, the story. There are four basic rules of anecdotal narration:

1. *Keep your events in natural sequence.* Don't backtrack. If we were writing about Jeff and the alarm clock, we might start out with something like this:

Last year, we had a hard time getting into the holiday spirit. Perhaps, we decided, the season would be more meaningful if we gave presents to people who otherwise would go without.

I asked the nurse at a middle school if she would find out what two or three disadvantaged youngsters would like for Christmas.

Two days later, she phoned. Debbie and Amanda, both 13, would like sweaters. Jeff, who was 12, wanted an alarm clock.

To be sure you have the events in order, write the incident down in chronological form:

our lack of spirit
decision to do something
contacting school nurse
getting information from nurse
running into nurse after Christmas
finding out that Jeff had given clock to his friend
punch line

2. *Don't overwrite or include extraneous details.* The nurse may have been discontented with her job, the school could have been in a slum neighborhood, Jeff might have been good in math. But don't include that information if it is not vital to your anecdote.
3. *Keep explanations simple and uncomplicated.* Explain just enough so the reader will catch the twist at the end.

In the Fritz Kreisler-Mrs. Vanderbilt anecdote, the principals were so well known that Cerf didn't have to explain who they were. He didn't have to spell out in detail that even Mrs. Vanderbilt thought five thousand dollars was a lot to pay for a Kreisler performance. In the alarm clock anecdote, you don't have to explain which other family members were in on the decision to give the gifts or to point out that the reason Jeff was poor was that his single parent was an alcoholic.

4. *Write the last line so that it has punch.* Rearrange words to
achieve the maximum impact, working with them until you
get just what you want. Though the meaning would have
been the same, if Cerf's last line had read "Well, if I don't
have to talk to your guests I'll only charge you two thousand
dollars for performing," its sparkle would have fizzled.

Description. Description, due to the brevity of the anecdotal
form, must be used sparingly, with short "tags" or descriptive adjectives telling about the people in the story or its setting. Don't
describe anything unessential to the story.

Imagery. Imagery is the use of words to paint verbal pictures,
allowing the reader to "see" the action. One of the most touching
anecdotes I've come across is "The Gracious Art of Taking—and
Giving," by B. Keith Cossey, which appeared in *Guideposts* two
decades ago. It's a story that is extremely well crafted, with a message that is timeless. As you read it, study the effective use of
imagery.

> My Marine buddy and I were taking a lunch break, eating our
> rations on the steps of an improvised medical clinic that we were
> helping set up for Vietnamese civilians. Patients milled around us
> and we had almost finished our meal before we noticed the small,
> frail boy who was watching us intently.
>
> He was about 11, and it was clear that he was being treated for
> malnutrition. We knew he was hungry. But he was not begging—
> just looking at us with friendly curiosity.
>
> My partner and I glanced at each other, then walked over to the
> child and offered him the only food we had left, one of the round
> chocolate disks that fits in the bottom of a C-ration can.
>
> Wordlessly, with narrow hands, the boy accepted the gift, then
> carefully broke it into three equal pieces. Placing one in my hand
> and one in my buddy's, he bowed the impeccably gracious Vietnam-
> ese bow and slipped away.

With each paragraph of this piece, I get a series of mental images. I have been on enough military bases and watched sufficient

television to picture the medical clinic. (In my mind's eye it's pale-green concrete, but that doesn't matter; each of us can respond with images arising from our particular experiences.) I've never been to Vietnam, but I have seen enough Vietnamese people and pictures to visualize the setting.

The words "small, frail boy," simple as they are, convey an image that works on my visual sense, as does the description of the malnourished child in the subsequent paragraph. I can see the two marshmallow-tough Marines, the C-ration chocolate (I'm sure it's a bit stale and slightly grey around the edges), the narrow hands, and the child bowing. The anecdote wouldn't be so moving if it did not prompt those mental pictures.

Dialogue: The Impact of Closing Statements. The easiest endings to write are those that involve dialogue, as illustrated by this typical *Catholic Digest* anecdote called "God Squad," written by Kathleen T. Choi.

After my conversion, my non-Christian husband found many Catholic practices puzzling. He teased me about terms like Easter duty and day of obligation.

"Don't tell me you believe you'll go to hell if you miss Mass," he protested.

I tried to explain that keeping spiritually healthy has its laws, just as physical health does, but he remained unimpressed.

Finally, however, I found an explanation my sports-buff spouse could understand. When the next holy day rolled around, I said to him, "You know the team I joined? Well, the Coach has called an extra practice."

In most anecdotes, the final action must carry the wallop. This becomes especially effective when the ending involves a reversal from what is expected, as in this anecdote from *Reader's Digest*. It was submitted by Cynthia L. Osburn and included with two other anecdotes under the heading "Senior Sparkle."

My grandmother, a feisty 91 and living alone in a small Missouri town, had a total hip replacement and was housebound.

Our family, not being nearby, was concerned for her welfare and called Meals on Wheels. My aunt let the service know of Grandmother's aversion to being thought helpless, so would they bring up the idea tactfully?

The next day a volunteer phoned Grandmother and cheerfully explained that Meals on Wheels is a service that relies on volunteers to help the elderly and the ill. Would she be interested in it?

There was a reflective pause. "Well, sure," my grandmother said. "If you can't find anyone else to get food to the old people, I guess *I* can."

A NOTE ON STRUCTURE

If you want to learn to craft first-rate anecdotes, those printed in *Reader's Digest* will serve you well as models. Most *Digest* anecdotes are composed of three parts. The first sentences introduce the characters and the situation or problem. The middle section describes the action or expands on the conflict. The anecdote closes with a satisfying ending, usually a punch line or twist that catches the reader off balance. The following *Reader's Digest* anecdotes, divided into these three parts, illustrate this structure:

One

In the admitting office of our hospital, some patients were filling out forms, others were being interviewed and still others were being escorted to their rooms.

Two

An elderly woman hesitantly entered my cubicle. She had completed her admitting forms and, upon my request, handed me her insurance cards. I typed the necessary information and then asked her the reason for her coming to the hospital.

Three

"Just to visit a friend," she said, "but this has taken so long, I'm not sure I have time now."

— Contributed by Mildred A. Hays

One

When West Valley College at Saratoga, Calif., staged *Jesus Christ Superstar*, the drama was enhanced by mysterious mists and zigzag lights. Blue clouds billowed across the scenery as the music soared.

Two

The cast looked surprised when sudden laughter from the audience broke the spell. It seems that a lighting technician had been creating the cloud effects by projecting a blue light through a glass bowl filled with water.

Three

The technique worked beautifully until on the backdrop, in distinct, king-sized letters, there appeared the word "Pyrex."

—Contributed by Charis Wright

One

As seniors, we were immersed in planning for life after graduation: résumés, interviews and making good impressions. Our professor told us about a friend who had used a creative approach applying for a job. He had studied up on the firm and was granted an interview in another city.

Two

On the big day, he arrived in a clean T-shirt, jeans and sneakers. When questioned about his unusual attire, he responded that he wanted to impress them with himself, not his clothes. The next time they saw him, he said, he would be wearing a suit. He was hired.

Three

We all marveled at his bravery and ingenuity. A classmate asked the professor how the fellow had come up with such a brilliant plan.

"It was simple," our professor replied. "On his trip to the interview, the airline lost his luggage."

—Contributed by Christine Sjolander

As you can see, the first example is written in first person and relates to an incident experienced by the anecdote's author. The second anecdote describes what happened to a group of people and is cast in the third person. The author could have been a part of the production or in the audience, but wouldn't necessarily have had to be present.

The third little story is a combination of first person plural and third person singular — a somewhat unusual mix for anecdotes but one that can be very effective.

Notice how dependent all three anecdotes are on imagery. It's so easy to visualize the elderly woman in the first story, looking quite bewildered when she's asked so many questions. And can't you just see the word PYREX floating through wispy clouds?

Each of the stories progresses naturally and leads up to such punchy last lines that it's easy to see why they beat out thousands of competitors.

You may not have worked in a hospital admitting office or taken classes from professors who illustrated their lectures with great stories, but you have had other experiences rich with anecdotal material. Learn to package them well and editors will come to depend on you for your stories.

MEASURING THE MARKETS

The anecdote market, as far as most writers are concerned, is *Reader's Digest*. It has the highest visibility and prestige of the publications that use little stories. Moreover, the *Digest* uses a lot of anecdotes in each issue and pays handsomely for them — you can make as much as $5 a word.

But the average writer's chances of selling to *Reader's Digest* are very slim indeed. According to its editors, 25,000 submissions arrive monthly for the combined humor features ("Laughter is the Best Medicine" and "Campus Comedy" are two of the most popular departments listed at the front of each issue). You'll rarely find more than two dozen anecdotes in an issue.

I don't want to discourage you from trying to snag that money. By all means submit if you have an anecdote idea that's strong enough to brave the competition and you've given the idea every possible chance by polishing each phrase so that it gleams like wedding-present silver.

I do suggest, however, that while you're waiting by the mailbox, you also try other anecdote markets. They don't pay as well, to be sure, but your submissions won't be battling the horrendous odds against acceptance.

No other markets print as many anecdotes as *Reader's Digest*. But neither are they as demanding. Your prose need not be as perfect, your story not so unusual or moving to make a sale at most of them.

The downside of anecdote writing is that market research takes a disproportionate amount of time, since only a few of the magazines listed in *Writer's Market* specify their need for anecdotes, though they might use them. So the most successful method of researching the markets is by looking out for the little stories in every magazine you see. Also, unlike a magazine's short takes, which are usually gathered together in one or two departments, anecdotes are frequently sprinkled throughout the publication.

To give you ideas, I'll tell you how I gained my knowledge of anecdote markets. By leafing through all of the tabloids at the supermarket checkout stand, for example, I've found that one of them—*Globe*—buys anecdotes on a regular basis. Among the women's magazines I've checked out while I'm waiting for the checker to check me out, *Redbook* and *Woman's World* can be counted on to use an anecdote or two in every issue.

In a Laundromat last summer, I found a pile of *Catholic Digests* and borrowed them overnight. They're great anecdote markets, I discovered, especially for people who think along religious lines. It becomes obvious upon reading several of the editors' previous choices that it's not necessary to be a Roman Catholic to succeed. Several of the anecdotes were strictly secular and might fit in a number of publications. Those in a religious vein usually could have been crafted by any writer who remembers to write "mass" instead of "church."

Whenever I travel to other parts of the country, I browse

through the magazines at newsstands and buy those I am not familiar with. That's how I found out that *Down East Magazine* publishes an "It Happened Down East" anecdote in each issue.

And so it goes with every magazine I can lay my hands on — fraternal, motor club, trade journal. Every time I find a market, I tear out the page (or photocopy it) and identify it as to magazine and date if that information isn't printed on the page.

Dating any material you clip from magazines is important, because editors can change their formats, deleting some departments, adding new ones, or the publication may have acquired a new editor since the material was clipped.

STICKING TO THE SUBJECT

The same anecdote, unlike most other short forms, may be suitable for several publications. Generally, however, minor alterations are in order.

Cute little stories about children are a case in point. When you find kiddie anecdotes in publications for seniors, the children are usually referred to as "my five-year-old grandson, Kyle" or "my three-year-old granddaughter." If the anecdotes are religion-related, be sure the setting — cathedral, synagogue, Sunday school, catechism class — is compatible with the particular magazine's religious persuasion.

A few publications have requirements that make anecdotes that are right for them unsuitable for most publications. For example, the anecdotes in *Globe* are longer than those you'll find in most magazines and are part of a department called "Candid Confessions." A boxed message on the middle of the page asks, "Do you have a deep, dark secret you'd like to share with GLOBE readers? Write and tell us about it. . . ." The anecdotes, with titles like "My love tub affair got boss in hot water," and "I bared underwear to set stage for revenge," aren't usually as titillating as the headings suggest. In fact, some of them deal with subjects like dropping food on the floor, scooping it up and serving it to unsuspecting guests.

As you would imagine, anecdotes in motor club magazines

relate to automobile travel; those in sports publications, to sports (either as a participant or spectator).

Which reminds me. Did you ever hear the little story about the writer who . . . ?

THE 30-MINUTE WRITER'S PLAN OF ACTION

1. Idea generating

A. Make lists of jobs you've had; interesting/good/out-of-the-ordinary-neighbors, friends and associates; places you've lived in and visited.

B. Use each item on your list to prompt your memory, recalling associated incidents: the neighbor who let her children write all over the walls so they could "express themselves"; the crazy excuse the plumber who fixed your disposal gave for being late; what the gunrunner's girlfriend said to you in the London hotel lobby.

C. Put together a file of potential markets, with examples of anecdotes their editors have bought in the past.

D. Pair up your ideas with these markets, then choose one that seems most likely to succeed and start on it first.

E. Make a chronological list of the events in your chosen story.

F. Try to think of the punch line first. If you get that, writing the rest of the little story is a lot easier.

CHAPTER XV

Prose

A String of Pearls
Act II, Scene One
Time: A Year or Two Later

Your thirty-minute scraps of time, stitched together, have produced a portfolio full of clippings, some of them bylined; others not. But they were all created by *you*.

You've overcome fear of rejection. And when people ask you what you do, your voice doesn't sound at all tentative as you tell them you're a writer.

It's time, perhaps, to think of using the thirty-minute segments to put together some larger works—feature articles, regular columns, even books.

And there's no doubt that you can do it.

My first dozen sales were shorties, most of them 400 to 700 words, none of them longer than 1,000. I simply did not have the courage or faith in my ability to attempt anything longer.

As I became more competent and confident, I began writing feature articles and books. Most published writers tell the same story.

So, let's examine the three most obvious types of longer works—feature articles, columns and books—to determine how they may fit into your writing life.

THE MAIN FEATURE

Feature articles in today's magazines generally run from 1,000 to 1,500 words—not that much longer than the pieces you've been writing. But in short takes, you only have words enough to tell about a tiny sliver of the subject pie—just the barest essentials about a new kind of tanning lotion or a recently discovered painting by Van Gogh. And in short articles and miniprofiles you're also working with a narrow focus. The full-blown feature requires more research, more interviews and, above all, more organization.

The transition to longer pieces, however, shouldn't be difficult for the 30-Minute Writer who has learned to use disconnected segments of time effectively. At the outset, you will need to spend some time evaluating the breadth of your idea to determine whether it is "big" enough to support an article of the length your prospective editor uses.

Perhaps in the course of writing certain short takes you've wished for more words, because there was much more to tell; or maybe the subjects of some of your miniprofiles were multifaceted people about whom you could have written pages more if you'd had the space. If so, you'll only need to augment the material you already have to produce full-length features.

After you've come up with a covey of ideas and paired them with potential markets, start writing query letters (for information on how to write good ones, see *How to Write Irresistible Query Letters*, Writer's Digest Books, 1990). Although most of the short forms we've covered in this book don't require letters of inquiry, the time-efficient writer uses them whenever possible before writing longer pieces, since it saves time and postage. There's no point in sending a completed manuscript to an editor who might already have a similar piece in the works or who would like the idea if only it were approached from another angle.

Usually, the most receptive editors to approach at the outset will be those you've sold short pieces to in the past. That is, if your material fits their publications. Be realistic. Aim for markets that will take the credits you've listed in your query letter seriously. If your published work has been in two or three magazines that pay five cents a word, don't try to take *Woman's Day* or *Conde Nast Traveler* by storm. Their writers have put in years of apprenticeship writing for other magazines. Instead, try periodicals that are on a par or just a bit up from those that have published your work.

When you receive a go-ahead, either on assignment or on speculation, your 30-Minute Writer skills at researching, interviewing and organization only need to be expanded. And whenever you are in doubt as to basic structure and style, look at back issues of the publication you're writing for.

ONCE-A-WEEK PIECES

Though good columns are so easy to read, becoming a columnist is hard. It takes imagination, persistence and staying power—a venture not to be taken lightly. If you're able to develop an idea that sells the editor, you will have taken on a responsibility that has to be fulfilled come hell, high water or sinus headache. But many writers who started out with only fragments of writing time have gone on to become successful columnists.

First, of course, you have to come up with a concept that you can sustain for weeks, months and, one hopes, years. I deliberately didn't mention daily, for no one of sound mind starts out by writing a daily column unless that's the only thing he or she plans to do and unless he or she has a guarantee of being well paid for the effort.

Many of the column concepts are already taken, at least on the big publication levels. Maybe your local newspaper could use a column on food or gardening or travel, but few other newspapers or magazines can. That is, unless you have an angle—perhaps hydroponic gardening or travel for the physically impaired—that doesn't overlap what the publication already runs.

Or perhaps you're thinking of something more exotic, such as hydroponically growing the out of the ordinary (minivegetables or carnivorous plants maybe) or traveling by unusual means of transportation (dhow, camel, wagon train). The problem here is that it would be difficult, time-consuming and expensive to gather material for three or four columns, let alone a year's worth. So do a thorough job of investigating your theme before you commit.

Looking ahead to column longevity and broad readership,

you'll want to spend a good deal of your time and imagination at the outset dreaming up a super theme or a fresh approach to one that's already popular. If you yearn to write a personal column, spend your up-front time thinking of a number of topics and work on deciding what style you'll use.

There are several factors that will influence the kinds of ideas you consider, among them your interests, areas of expertise, your way with words, your sense of humor. If you're a whiz at computers and find it easy to explain complicated subjects so that even your airhead friends can understand them, or if you're passionately interested in contemporary music, you have several column choices that complement those qualities.

If you can put a clever spin on everyday occurrences, find humor in shopping malls, appliance salesmen's pitches, adult education classes, and taking out the garbage, you're probably a natural for a personal column.

Successful columnists use a variety of techniques for ongoing idea generation. People who write informational columns read voraciously about their subjects and have a bevy of other experts with whom they keep in close touch. Top columnists who write about entertaining haunt the florists, homeware departments, fabric and craft stores; they talk to caterers, celebrities and specialty food suppliers. They're always the first to read the newly released books on their subject and wherever they go are on the lookout for new trends and ideas.

Writers of personal columns may make lists of peoples' basic and perceived needs, such as food, shelter, clothing, health, relationships and entertainment as a starting point, then couple them with trendy topics. Or they may go through newspapers, with an eye to human interest angles. Some writers make lists of unusual occupations or of everyday items and activities like soap, transparent tape, washing the car, wrapping gifts.

Some mix and match their lists—cookware with antiques, springtime with stress. They read tabloids, travel brochures, toothpaste ads, the "People Patterns" department in the *Wall Street Jour-*

nal, the state-by-state briefs in *USA Today*. They watch TV news and game shows like "Jeopardy."

Once you've decided what kind of a column to write, get to work and put together a half-dozen of them, even before you have a buyer. Perhaps some of the short articles you have written can be adapted. Maybe you'll write them from scratch. But be sure they're your best work.

As far as style is concerned, unless you're writing a medical or political column — and often, even if you are — you'll want to keep your tone conversational. If you think about it, reading your favorite columnist is like having a chat with a cherished friend. Warmth, compassion, a sense of humor — especially when its directed at oneself — all are ingredients that good writers use to achieve this reader rapport. By going public with their innermost feelings, they achieve a "me, too" effect, letting us know that they blush when they're embarrassed, that they have feelings of insecurity, and that they take pride in their minor triumphs just like we do.

After you've written your sample columns, the next step is to get your material in the hands of editorial decision makers. Many people start with their local newspapers, which is a good training ground if the person who edits copy knows his or her job. But your material may be better suited to a magazine, ideally one to which you've already sold short pieces of work and established your reliability.

SYNDICATION: THE COLUMNIST'S DREAM

Only after you've sold your column and written it regularly for a reasonable period of time can you begin to think about syndication. And thinking may be all you want to do. For selling your column to a syndicator is a difficult job. Many are submitted but very few are chosen.

Self-syndication can require your full-time efforts, and even then you may not succeed. It can also cost a great deal in photocopying costs, mailing supplies and postage to get started.

Being as objective as possible, ask yourself a number of questions before you even consider approaching a syndicator or embarking on the adventure of doing it yourself. Among them are:

1. Does your material have broad reader interest, appealing to both sexes, to people of all age groups, educational levels, occupations, economic levels?
2. Will your material interest anyone besides its present readership? It may be a howl in Three Forks, Montana, but will it play in Peoria?
3. Is the material easy to read and understand? Is it interesting, informative and/or entertaining?
4. Does it have emotional appeal, or is it genuinely funny?
5. Is the title catchy?
6. Are you willing to stick with the project, despite lack of economic encouragement, for a period of months or years?
7. If the project takes off, are you interested enough to keep writing the column for an extended period of time?

If you can answer most of the questions affirmatively, your next step is deciding whether to approach a syndicator or to attempt to syndicate the material yourself. If you decide on the first course, package copies of ten to twenty of your best published columns, send the packages to a number of syndicators, and follow up each submission with a personal call or telephone conversation.

If your material is accepted for syndication, don't rush right out and buy a BMW. Syndicated columnists don't become millionaires overnight. Most don't become millionaires ever.

Syndication companies act as agents, packaging your work, sending it off to their customers, and splitting the fees with you, usually 50-50. You don't get much money per column per newspaper, but if a number of publications choose your work, the figures become impressive.

This sounds great, especially if the syndicate sells to 1,500 papers like the Los Angeles Times Syndicate. But the bottom line is that not every customer buys everything a syndicate wants to sell them. Some columns grow in popularity; others fizzle.

Self-syndication also starts with preparation packages containing previously published columns, but you put together a great many more packages and send them yourself to newspapers and other publications that use syndicated material. How many packages you send depends upon the amount of money you're willing to spend. People who have self-syndicated say that if you get one acceptance out of ten submissions, you'll be doing well.

IF THEY ASKED ME, I COULD WRITE A BOOK—MAYBE

And now, we've come to books. But let's not abandon the subject of columns just yet, because many of the most popular books of the past have consisted of previously published columns. Many of these books haven't required any additional words from their authors other than those in the Introduction.

Whether columns or not, most collections/anthologies weren't written in one fell swoop. Erma Bombeck, Robert Fulghum, Art Buchwald, and scores of other authors didn't produce their best-sellers until they had written lots of little bits—columns or sermons or short articles that were later gathered together and edited.

Not all of these collections are made up entirely of previously published material, however. In some cases, the authors must write additional chapters and rewrite parts of others to round out their books' contents or provide unifying themes. But this sort of piecemeal writing also lends itself to the 30-Minute Writer's M.O.

Whenever you don't think you can do it, leaf through a book by any of the above. Taken section by section, the prospect of writing all the words necessary for even a long work doesn't seem so daunting.

I have Fulghum's *All I Really Need to Know I Learned in Kindergarten* in front of me now. None of the observations is longer than 1,000 words. Like the pieces in Bombeck's and Buchwald's books, the subject matter is both ordinary and imaginative. Ordinary in that most of the pieces are about everyday things/events, imaginative in the way the authors treat them.

Fulghum, in the first of his best-sellers, talks about everything from jumper cables to rip-off artists; children's games to the Spanish conquistador-priests. Not a world-shaking subject in the book. They don't have to be.

Granted, most of us won't ever be Bombecks or Fulghums or Buchwalds. But maybe a few of us will. For once we've become successful 30-Minute Writers, we can stretch ourselves to produce more time-consuming successes. We can even write 300-page books from scratch.

Often, books are written because their authors happened upon a tiny bite of information and pursued it until they had reams of notes. One of the small pieces you've written could be such an informational starter, or it might be that snippet of trivia you couldn't resist copying down while researching another piece.

Marketing your book is explained in depth in *How to Write a Book Proposal* (Writer's Digest, 1990). Usually, the process consists of querying editors by letter, briefly describing the book and/or sending along a multipage outline and two or three sample chapters. This involves a considerable outlay of time, but it's difficult for a writer who hasn't had any books published to gain acceptance without following the prescribed procedure.

Wherever your inspiration for a book begins, remember that you only need to write it one chapter at a time. And experienced 30-Minute Writers know that writing one chapter is no more than the cumulative production of a number of half-hour sessions — at the library, at interviews, at the word processor — put together. So book writing is definitely among the projects that a 30-Minute Writer who has been at it for a time should think about undertaking. It's not easy, but it can be done.

This book is a case in point. I signed the contract for it shortly before our Marine Reserve son came back from Saudi Arabia. In the following six months, I became involved in self-contracting an extensive remodeling project, at times with electricians, plumbers and four carpenters on the job.

Meanwhile, there were two national cook-offs to participate in, dozens of other contests to enter, another book proposal to write, article assignment deadlines to be met, visits to and from family and friends, meals to be made, shopping and cleaning to be done. I rarely had a stretch of uninterrupted time at the word processor that lasted longer than half an hour.

While I hope you won't have such a horrendous case of occupational overload with so many different irons in the writing fire, you may have. Just don't let it stop you.

Now, you may think that it's hard to sustain momentum and interest with so many interruptions. I've found that it's just the opposite. Writing time, interspersed with other tasks, gives me the change of pace that generates enthusiasm.

I can't wait to get back to the word processor, but the thought of sitting there for eight solid hours and having to justify the time spent with pages of copy, on the other hand, gives me the willies. In fact, I'm sure that long writing stretches are one of the main contributors to writer's block.

However, I realize that some people may lose momentum and interest because of the interruptions. And I'd be less than honest if I claimed that losing interest isn't sometimes a problem with any work, whether it is 500 or 500,000 words long.

When this happens in a longer work, you might begin writing the segment that's easiest. Getting something—anything—done will propel you forward. You might think of how great your name will look on the book cover or how wonderful you'll feel on your way to the bank. Promise yourself a treat when you've finished five pages. Read a good book and imagine the process, as well as the satisfaction, of writing it. Do anything to rekindle the writing flame.

PUTTING THEORY TO PRACTICE

Now that we've explored the longer writing forms in general, let's begin with chapter two and do a chapter-by-chapter reprise to see more specifically how little pieces can lay the groundwork or form the actual basis for longer works of the same kind.

Chapter Two. You decided early on that you liked writing (and were successful at placing) short takes. Several of them, it turns out, were about clever products dreamed up and marketed by youngsters. A number of others were about unusual celebrations.

What about writing a full-length feature on young entrepreneurs, and one about out-of-the-ordinary celebrations throughout the country, using the material you already have as nuclei for the articles?

Chapter Three. One-pagers have proven to be your favorites. You especially like having at least 800 words to work with. For you, it's an easy transition to writing longer articles. You shouldn't be intimidated at all, especially when you realize that most feature articles today run about 1,500 words and hardly ever contain more than 2,500. All you need do is look at the longer pieces as two or three short ones with a common subject.

Loriann Hoff Oberlin, who juggles being a newsletter editor, public relations consultant, wife and mother with her freelancing, makes big writing jobs seem smaller by dividing them into logical segments. When she finishes one, she starts on the next. "I only think about one part of the piece at a time," she says.

Chapter Four. Likewise, if your specialty has become short profiles: The writing will be the same; there will just be more of it. The increased amount of research required should pose no great problems, either. You'll probably have to spend more than thirty minutes interviewing your central figure, but most of the corollary interviews—business associates, family members, former lovers, potential competitors—should fit into the thirty-minute framework (remember, if you establish a friendly rapport, your interviewees won't usually object to follow-up phone calls).

To begin with, you may want to build on work you've already done. Perhaps you have written a series of articles about small hotels or private yachts or crazy contests. By writing a lead and stringing the pieces together with only a few words of transition, you'll have a full-blown feature article.

Chapter Five. The op-ed technique, per se, is a bit harder to parlay into larger works, but only because issues and topics become dated so quickly. However, if you choose timely subjects, buttress your opinions with those of experts in the field. By planning on about twice as much writing time as you needed for your opinion pieces, you should be able to write full-length features or even a regular column expressing your opinionated views, such as that Barbara Grizzuti Harrison writes for *Mademoiselle.*

Who knows, after you sell a number of op-ed pieces to the same publication, its editors may be calling to say "Would you like to?"

Chapter Six. You have no doubt found if you have decided to become a humorist that it's hard to stay funny for 750 words, let alone 1,500. That's why most humorous articles are shorter than 1,000 words. A collection of humorous pieces, however, can be the beginning of a regular column or a book.

Furthermore, if you are adept at humor, you'll have a laugh on the competition since most articles can use a few—or a lot of— smiles tucked in with the information.

Chapter Seven. Hints and Tipsters' natural evolutionary path is to writing how-to articles. If you can solve little problems, you can find out how to handle the bigger ones. As for the hints and tips themselves, you only have to look to Mary Ellen and Heloise for examples of how they've been parlayed into big bucks.

Chapter Eight. A natural for you will be the inspirational roundup feature, popular in so many women's and general interest magazines. They usually consist of three to five inspirational stories—all with a common thread—about ordinary people who have done the near-heroic. These pieces may be about people who have overcome physical disabilities, fought to save their communities, inaugurated programs for the disadvantaged, or done anything else that will inspire the publication's readers. If you're putting the piece together for a regional publication, finding the people to write about won't be difficult. It's harder, however, for a national market because you'll want to have a good geographical mix—the young mother in Connecticut, wheat farmer in Kansas, retiree in California sort of combination.

Your best markets will again be publications to which you've already sold, provided they use material of the sort you propose to write. Whatever editors you decide to query, be sure to enclose copies of your previously published inspirationals if they're in the same style you plan to use.

Chapter Nine. A restaurant review column in local or regional publications is the obvious offshoot of the kind of writing you've been doing. But there are other possibilities. You can do roundups of restaurants in popular tourist destinations for a variety of magazines, including those focusing on travel as well as food and drink.

Or how about putting together some appetizing queries on things to eat? After gaining food-writing experience by doing restaurant reviews, I sold pieces on oysters, cheese and cranberries to airline in-flight magazines. Writing about food festivals is yet another option.

Chapter Ten. Editors of magazines that use personal essays tell me that they often have trouble finding good material. That's why some of them have contracted with writers to provide the essays on a regular basis. If you can establish a writer/editor relationship based on your performance as a skillful and reliable producer, ask about becoming a personal essayist whose work appears in every issue.

Another possibility, provided you feel you'd like to write personal essays forever, is to take the best of those you've already written and approach editors about writing a regular column for them.

Chapter Eleven. Regular columns on music, art, theater, books; feature articles critical of some process, plan or product; books dissecting anything from health care ethics to automobile marketing in the United States—the accomplished reviewer has a choice of many directions. Developing a critical eye and establishing a reputation for knowing what you are talking about are bankable assets with editors you have sold to in the past, and they're good training for future endeavors.

Chapter Twelve. Is there a writer's life after contesting? If it's still a struggle to compose your recipes after entering a year's worth of contests, the answer is probably "no." But if you find you like putting the words on paper as well as you like putting the ingredients together in the kitchen, the opportunities are there.

I've heard of contest winners who have gone on to become food editors and cookbook writers. Or maybe you'll talk the editor of the local paper into a contesting column. One word of warning, however. Such ventures may cause you to lose your amateur cook status and make you ineligible to enter most cooking contests in the future.

Chapter Thirteen. People who write articles and create activities for children's publications find it an easy transition to move on to nonfiction books for the same age group. If you decide to follow this path, you'll want to devise a strategy for successful marketing. Talk to a children's librarian who can tell you which kinds of books are most popular, citing specifics. Pore over catalogs of children's books and the children's section of *Books in Print*. Talk to booksellers and schoolteachers to find out what book they'd like to find, but can't because it hasn't been written yet. Then *write it*.

Chapter Fourteen. By learning to craft anecdotes, you have mastered one of the most valuable tools in the writer's kit. In larger works, you can use them as leads, to illustrate points, and as closings—adding the touches of human interest that editors love. Since anecdotal style is extremely popular, capitalize on your skill in whatever writing forms you choose.

ADVANCED IDEA GENERATION

By the time you're achieving success as a 30-Minute Writer, your idea-making mechanism should be going into high gear. In fact, every once in a while you'll be inclined to ask your brain to turn off the idea machine. Don't.

What you want to do, instead, is to become more efficient in your idea generating and evaluating techniques. For one thing, you'll have developed strong opinions on what subjects you *don't* want to write about. You'll also have a better handle on the kinds of pieces you write that sell best. You may have wrestled with— and settled—the question of whether you want to be a specialist or a generalist. In other words, since you've come to know yourself as a writer, you can work to select your ideas accordingly.

A natural progression that follows this insight into your writing strengths is the cultivation of compatible idea sources. You'll attend meetings and seminars on subjects that dovetail with your areas of interest, read specialized publications, talk with experts on the cutting edge of the kinds of innovations you write best about. True writers don't sit around waiting for inspiration. They go where the ideas are.

ADVANCED MARKETING

As your thirty-minute successes pile up in the "Published" file, you'll also find that your reading patterns may change. The discretionary time you used to spend absorbed in novels may now be transferred to devouring *Publishers Weekly* or poring over articles on publishing and advertising in the *Wall Street Journal*.

In the process, you'll become a more sophisticated marketer of your writing wares. Information about magazines currently being tested in "charter" or "pilot" issues; gossip about publications that are in financial trouble; news about monthlies that are planning to put out additional issues will all add to your body of publishing knowledge. You will be more aware of specialization trends, of what the public wants, of what magazines are looking for.

An example of this kind of advance knowledge was buried in a January 8, 1991, *Wall Street Journal* article. It said that *Parenting Magazine* was contemplating an extra issue during the year that would focus on travel. The 30-Minute Writer interested in doing articles about kids and travel would waste no time in working up a couple of on-target queries to the magazine's editor.

Another publication you might want to add to your pile of bedside reading is *Advertising Age*. Each issue of *Ad Age* contains little jewels such as the publications certain manufacturers, departments of tourism and the like plan to place ads in as part of upcoming campaigns. It also reports when the larger companies change ad agencies and public relations firms. I clip these items, since it's great to have on file when you want to save time getting info on a specific product or place.

AND YET ANOTHER OPTION

Just because you've succeeded as a 30-Minute Writer doesn't mean that you want to go on to longer works. Shorter may mean better in your life. You may have a regular job that you like. Or you might hate your job, look forward to quitting, but you have a mind that likes to explore lots and lots of things; that doesn't want to take the time to find out about them in depth.

Good News! You don't have to write feature articles or columns or books to be a writing success. It's quite possible to make more money per hour writing the short stuff. I know. There have been periods in my life when I've done just that.

The most important thing for anyone who likes to write is to find the writing-world niche that's most comfortable for him or her. Since it's such a diverse occupation, there's room for everyone with desire and a willingness to work at their chosen craft. Thousands of 30-Minute Writers have found their special place. You will, too.

Index